Feelings

To David Ray Griffin

Feelings

Charles Birch

**UNSW
PRESS**

Published by
UNIVERSITY OF NEW SOUTH WALES PRESS
Sydney 2052 Australia
Telephone (02) 398 8900   Fax (02) 398 3408

© 1995 Charles Birch
First printed in 1995

National Library of Australia
Cataloguing-in-Publication entry:

Birch, Charles, 1918– .
Feelings.

  Bibliography.
  Includes index.
  ISBN 0 86840 151 X.

  1. Consciousness. 2. Emotions. 3. Neurophysiology –
  Philosophy. 4. Mind and body.

152.4

Typeset in Bembo 11.4/13.6pt
Printed by Southwood Press

Available in North America through:
ISBS Inc
Portland Oregon 97213-3644
Tel: (503) 287 3093
Fax: (503) 280 8832

CONTENTS

We live in deeds, not years; in thoughts, not breaths;
In feelings, not in figures on a dial.
We should count time by heart-throbs. He most lives
Who thinks most — feels the noblest — acts the best.

PHILIP JAMES BAILEY, FESTUS, V

The angel's spear plunged into my heart several times, so that it
penetrated my entrails...the pain was so great that I screamed
aloud, but simultaneously felt such infinite sweetness that I
wished the pain to last eternally.

ST TERESA OF AVILA, IN HER ECSTASY

ACKNOWLEDGMENTS

David Ray Griffin and John B. Cobb Jr read the complete manuscript of this book and both gave me much helpful advice and criticism for which I am extremely grateful. It gives me great pleasure to dedicate this book to David Griffin, not only because he has been a major influence in the development of my ideas, but also because he has been a trailblazer in developing a panexperientialist view of the world in his many papers and books. He is a philosopher who brings science, philosophy and religion together in a constructive postmodern worldview. I also express gratitude to Peter Farleigh who gave me much advice and criticism for Chapter 4, about which he knows much more than I do, and Warwick Fox who provided me with much helpful information on the unconscious mind for Chapter 1. Julia Collingwood provided me with a number of helpful suggestions in the early stages of writing and has always been a most gracious and efficient adviser. I am indebted to Carl Harrison-Ford for his meticulous, imaginative and understanding editing.

INTRODUCTION

'The difficulty of keeping body and soul together', 'From soul to software', 'The nerve cell of the soul', 'The astonishing hypothesis' are all headlines of popular articles on the relation of the brain and feelings. There has recently been a spate of books by both biologists and philosophers on this subject. There are a number of reasons for this contemporary interest. One is that a number of famous scientists have, in the last decade or so, turned their research to neurophysiology, to try to discover the relation of brain and mind (which includes feelings), which is, at present, the greatest enigma of biology. Another reason is the claim of some exponents of artificial intelligence that the brain is to be understood as a computer. Doubtless both movements have stimulated philosophers to enter the debate on what some of them have called neurophilosophy. This is not just a dispute between academics. It has to do with questioning the very foundations of our feelings, our freedom, our sense of selfhood, human respect and moral decisions. Are these all illusions? Or are we in the process of discovering a new foundation for their reality?

In his book *The Astonishing Hypothesis: The Scientific Search for the Soul*, Nobel laureate Francis Crick tells us that our joys and sorrows, our memories and ambitions, our sense of personal identity and free will, are no more than the activity of a vast assembly of nerve cells and their associated molecules in the brain. Since 'this hypothesis is so alien to the ideas of most people alive today it can truly be called astonishing' says Crick. Astonishing or not, the hypothesis is not exactly new. I indicate, in Chapter 1, how the idea goes back to the ancient Greeks. I shall also argue that the hypothesis is astonishing in the sense that it is telling us that what matters most to each one of us, namely our feelings, hopes, ambitions and purposes are illusions. To argue that the only real things are atoms and molecules is materialism with a vengeance, cloaked in the most modern of modern science.

The claim of Crick, and others of this way of thinking, is that a final completely scientific and physical theory of the mind and all our feelings is inevitable and that we are well on the way to discovering it. The only real things are those objective entities we call atoms, cells and so on. Another way of putting this is to say that this school of thought has complete faith in reductionism. This is the belief that the living and the non-living are best understood in terms of their component building blocks such as atoms as described by physicists. 'I can call spirits from the vasty deep,' says Glendower to Hotspur in *Henry IV, Part 1*. 'Why so can I, or so can any man,' replies the latter; 'But will they come when you do call for them?' That is the question I put to Crick. In his critique of Crick's book, John Cornwell argues that Crick's formulation of the question is problematic and that what Crick regards as an unexceptionable starting point is not so reasonable as he would have us believe. 'In other words, is it reasonable to say that the best way to study a Rembrandt is to start by examining the molecules of paint on the canvas?' (Cornwell 1994, p. 829).

The inadequacy of oversimplified reductionism is sensed by the lay public. Unfortunately many of them turn to the appeal of the New Age antiscience. They deserve something better.

Reductionism in neurophysiology leads to a completely mechanical analysis of the brain. It is no exaggeration to say that most scientists simply do not know how to think about the world, and all that is in it, including brains, except in terms of machinery. They have yet to understand what Paul Davies and John Gribbin call 'the matter myth', which is the title of their book (Davies and Gribbin 1991). I have more to say about reductionism and mechanism and why I think they are inadequate in Chapter 3.

There are other ways of questioning nature besides reductionism. Indeed, as physicist Werner Heisenberg pointed out, 'what we observe is not nature in itself but nature exposed to our method of questioning' (Berman 1981, p. 145). This essential insight of modern science was stated with impressive brevity by Arthur Eddington:

> We have found that where science has progressed the farthest, the mind has but regained from nature that which the mind has

put into nature. We have found a strange footprint on the shores of the unknown. We have devised profound theories, one after another, to account for its origin. At last, we have succeeded in reconstructing the creature that made the footprint. And Lo! it is our own (Wilber 1984, p. 73).

In this sort of exercise, as in much of science, no one can pretend to offer proofs. What we can do is to offer plausibility, while at the same time recognising our own footprints in the sand.

I do not propose to deal in detail with all the different philosophies of consciousness. Instead I concentrate on the one which is most neglected and which I consider to be the most relevant. This alternative is a minority position at present. In addition to the objective reality of atoms, and all the rest that science investigates, there is a subjective reality which in ourselves we know as our feelings or our consciousness of, for example, pain when we break a leg, sorrow when we lose a loved one, or the joy of being in love. The proposition is that the subjective is as real as the objective. The task of this school is to tell us how the subjective is related to the objective. What, for example, is the connection between the objective information about chemical hormones and our *feelings* of being in love? This particular example is explored in Chapter 1. However, this point of view goes much further and says that what we know about consciousness in ourselves has parallels in all the individual entities of nature from people all the way down to protons. This proposition, which is discussed in Chapter 3, is known as panexperientialism. For the reader who wants a simple run-down of all alternative positions without the technical details I would suggest an essay by Colin McGinn (1993) which is really a discussion between McGinn and a visitor from outer space. Some of these alternative positions are discussed as we face them in subsequent chapters.

It has been said that Galileo's work in astronomy and physics was devoted to transforming 'the obviously ridiculous into the ridiculously obvious' (Gingerich 1994). The obviously ridiculous was the new cosmology that put the Sun instead of the Earth at the centre of the solar system. Copernicus and Galileo made this hypothesis ridiculously obvious. Likewise, prior to Charles

Darwin, the concept of biological evolution was, for most people, obviously ridiculous. With Darwin's theory of evolution by natural selection, the hypothesis became ridiculously obvious, so much so that Darwin's protagonist Thomas Henry Huxley exclaimed 'fancy not having thought of that before'.

In this book I try to show that what is obviously ridiculous to the materialist, namely the basic reality of feelings in nature, can become a ridiculously obvious hypothesis.

The astronomer Sir Fred Hoyle, remarking on the various problems as yet unresolved in cosmology, said that if a problem has an orthodox solution, the scientific community would already have found it. So for good reason, he said, he devoted much of his life to searching for unorthodox solutions to the problems of cosmology.

The reluctance to speculate freely on the limitations of traditional methods is a form of obscurantism. Indeed 'it is more than that', says Whitehead (1929), 'it is the negation of the importance of such speculation...The obscurantists of any generation are in the main constituted by the greater part of the practitioners of the dominant methodology' (pp. 43-4).

Science is not immune from this criticism, despite the fact that progress in science has involved great speculative jumps that led to experimentation and the revelation of new facts. The growth of science is like the growth of a crab that periodically results in the shedding of an old shell and the growth of a new one. This process is slow and painful. The old shell has served a good purpose and perhaps the crab is loath to part with such a hardened and protective structure. The traditional shell of the science and philosophy of consciousness (mechanism or materialism) has begun to crack. Some bits have already dropped off. Should this crab go on getting fat and take no thought for the raiment of the morrow? Or should it resolutely face the situation, heave off the remains of the old shell and set about making a new one in earnest? That day should not be delayed much longer. If it is put off too long the process of growth will suffer. Periods occur in the life of every branch of understanding when revision and stocktaking of its foundations become necessary. That was true of physics when the

Newtonian universe began to be superseded by Einstein's theory of relativity which was, in due course, modified by quantum theory. It is the case of the crab growing a new shell. Indeed the new shell of the new physics is radically different from anything that Newton believed. Instead of talking about a universe made up of particles of matter the new physics says there are no particles. There may not be any such thing as mass. What there is is more akin to energy and relationships than anything solid. That leads to the important question discussed in Chapter 3 as to what is there left to build the world-machine from once its atomic components have been dissolved into pools of energy, waves and relationships?

The situation today in the science of mind and feeling is that it needs to grow a new shell as physics has been doing in recent decades. A lot of what I have to say is to do with solid facts of contemporary biology presented in a new context that helps to make sense of our lives and that of other creatures. Traditional approaches to understanding feelings have got us only so far. One purpose of this book is to indicate what has been gained from tradition and how that tradition needs to be superseded.

1

Human Feelings

The expression of various feelings produces the history of mankind as distinct from the narrative of animal behaviours. History is the record of the expressions of feelings peculiar to humanity...The distinction between men and animals is in one sense only a difference in degree. But the extent of the degree makes all the difference. The Rubicon has been crossed.

A. N. WHITEHEAD (1966, p. 27)

By the middle of the twentieth century two major mysteries of ancient times — the nature of physical matter and the nature of living matter — were well on the way to be unravelled. At the same time, however, a third mystery that had also fascinated the ancients — the enigma of the human mind — had yet to achieve comparable clarification.

HOWARD GARDNER, QUOTED IN PAGELS (1988, p. 179)

Feelings are what matter most in life. Yet we are only now beginning to understand what feelings are and what produces them. Much of what scientists and philosophers claim to know is highly controversial. In the seventeenth century Descartes declared that mind and matter were two distinct sorts of things, though he was unable to tell us how they interacted. However, Descartes' dualism has now been almost totally discredited. Dualists still exist who yet admit that the problem of how mind and matter are related seems to be insoluble (e.g., Madell 1988). The current orthodoxy both in philosophy and in such fields as artificial intelligence (AI) or cognitive science is that what we call mind is totally explicable in materialistic or mechanistic terms. Hence the faith of strong AI that you can build a mind from little parts, each mindless in itself. This view is known as mechanism or physicalism. However, there are some physicalists who consider that the problem of the relation of mind and matter is insoluble (e.g., McGinn 1991; Seager 1991). One would think that the nest of problems that both dualism and physicalism raise might lead their proponents to search in another direction.

There is indeed an alternative to both dualism and physicalism that has been around for quite a long time (see Griffin 1995). It is a minority position that is less well known. It goes by various names such as psychicalism, panpsychism and panexperientialism. Its central idea is that mind and matter are not two different things but two aspects of the one thing, like the two sides of a coin. They are not two sorts of thing but one sort of thing. At the most fundamental levels of nature they are inseparable. This view is therefore opposed to the faith that you can build a mind from parts, each mindless in itself. Panexperientialism may be an astounding hypothesis but it is the view that makes the most sense to me and which I expound in this book. It takes very seriously the reality of feelings and the subjective in general to the extent of considering experience to be fundamental aspects of the basic entities in the cosmos, hence the pan in panexperientialism. This is basically a feeling universe — not a universe of machinery.

But why are our feelings important and why is it important that we have some understanding of their place in nature? I have a card on my desk which reminds me each day that 'To live with zest I have to be constantly challenged'. I want to live each day with zest. So at the beginning of each day I ask myself — what is the challenge of the day? There may be a list of things in my mind to be done or perhaps just one thing, completing some writing or maybe going for a picnic or talking with students. Zest is the feeling of excitement, creativity, strength, enthusiasm and passion. Zest is intensity of experience. It can be the new appreciation of a beautiful day in which sky and earth merge; catch it if you can as Cezanne said 'one minute in the life of the world is going by, paint it as it is'. Or it may be the excitement of adventure in a new project or a new friendship. It may be the excitement of new thoughts. 'Thoughts,' said Whitehead, 'are intellectual *feelings*.' All feelings, intellectual and otherwise, matter to me. They are what matter most.

Zest is at one end of the spectrum of human feelings. At the opposite end is depression, which is the lack of excitement, hope, creativity, strength and passion. It can even seem then that life is no longer worth living. It happens to some young people today who, for no fault of their own, cannot find employment. That can be a hell. 'All hope abandon, ye who enter here' is the inscription Dante saw written over the gates of hell. Among Australian males aged 15 to 24 years the suicide rate has more than trebled between 1950 and 1990 and in the nineties is amongst the highest in the world. Behind the problems of youth suicide, alcohol, drug abuse and delinquency are a constellation of traits of despondent feelings; hopelessness, loneliness and depression. For many young Australians, for much of the time, their feelings are anything but zestful. That such feelings are so common in our society matters a great deal.

Feelings of zest may last for a time to give way to the opposite. I stood at the edge of the Grand Canyon spellbound by its grandeur and beauty. I was alone. Quite suddenly I was overwhelmed by a feeling of a need to share the experience of awe with someone. My immediate feeling of awe was replaced by a strange feeling of loneliness.

My first adventure overseas was to spend a year and a half in the University of Chicago. For months before I ever got there I had feelings of great anticipation and adventure. Soon after my arrival I was overcome with quite another feeling of lostness and loneliness from being cut off from friends and a fear as to whether I had the capacity to do what I had set out to do in a foreign land.

Pretty well all popular songs have one subject only. It is the *feeling* of being in love. The lyrics usually don't say much but repeat again and again that this is a feeling no one would ever want to lose. For the addict, the promise of drugs is for a feeling the addict wants to have for ever. The promise is illusory and the price is high.

As A. N. Whitehead says, in the quotation at the head of this chapter, history is the expression of human feelings, be they of the heights or the depths of experience. There can hardly be more striking examples of this proposition than the lives of Hitler and Stalin and their effects on humanity, as documented by Alan Bullock's (1993) dual biography. The feelings of these two despots about life changed the history of humanity, as Bullock (1993) relates:

> The years I have recalled in this book showed, as perhaps never before, the depths of evil of which human beings are capable in their treatment of each other. But the historical record also shows that even in the worst circumstances, not only in battle but in overcrowded prisons and camps, under torture, in Resistance and in face of certain death, there was a handful — drawn from every nation — who showed to what heights men and women can rise…They remain for me, the double image of those years, the unbelievable cruelty and the courage, the callousness and the compassion — the human capacity for evil but also the reassurance of the possibility of nobility. (pp. 1063-4)

The future history of the world will be determined by the feelings of people alive today and the extent to which their feelings are deeply influenced by the terrible and the noble events of the past and as well by the indifference that can lead to sorrow. I picked up a postcard in a photographic exhibition of Nazi horror when in East Berlin recently. An East German friend translated these words on it by Elie Wiesel, a survivor of concentration camps:

The opposite of love is not hatred,
The opposite of hope is not despair,
The opposite of mental health is not madness,
The opposite of remembering is not forgetting,
In every case the opposite is nothing but indifference.

My feelings are with me all the time, even in my dreams when
I am asleep. Feelings are one of two fundamental traits of mind,
the other being willing. Feeling is the more fundamental of the
two. The dictionary says feelings are emotions, sensitivities, passions. Because I feel, I know that I am. So said Descartes. Willing
is purpose or determination. Knowing is also a trait of the mind
but is less fundamental in the sense that we can have feelings without conscious knowledge. Most of us think of feelings as always
being conscious, but a lot of our feelings are in the subconscious,
as I discuss later on. Willing and knowing are important. Their
importance to me is the feelings of creativity they engender. The
first point then is the importance of feelings. Feelings are what
matter most to each one of us, moment by moment, and the feelings of people down the ages determine history, age by age.

The flight from subjectivity

It is extraordinary that philosophers and psychologists have
been unable to agree as to what feelings are. Nor has science
had much to say about them until recently. John Searle (1992)
remarks that the principal goal of mainstream modern thought in
philosophy has been to exile feelings from the field of study, that
for the best part of a century professional philosophers have been
out to reduce consciousness to physical entities or activities and
finally to computation as in cognitive science. Likewise a generation of psychologists, under the influence of the behaviourist B. F.
Skinner, held back progress of human and animal psychology by
denying the existence of consciousness. As a wit of his day
remarked — psychology was losing consciousness.

Neurophysiologist Gerald Edelman (1992) thinks that science
hasn't done much better than philosophy and psychology, though
he hopes to change that. Science has evaded the mystery of subjectivity. It has failed to come clean about the objective/subjective

divide in our experience. Edelman goes so far as to say that this is 'the crisis of modern science'. Molecular biologist Francis Crick (1994) has faith that molecular biology applied to the brain will in due course provide a mechanistic answer to the problem of consciousness.

The argument for the reality of subjective feelings begins in this chapter and continues in Chapter 2. That leads to a discussion in Chapter 3 of a philosophy of life and view of science that rejects the flight from subjectivity and takes feelings to be the foundation of all that matters in a philosophy of life. This principle requires that we take as the basis of all our most fundamental concepts the fact of our own existence as experiencing subjects. This leads ineluctably to a philosophy quite distinct from that dominant in the classical tradition. Schubert Ogden (1967, p. 57) argues that the characteristics of classical philosophy all derive from the virtual exclusion of the phenomenon of experiencing persons. Instead it starts with the view that reality consists of chairs and tables and other objects we perceive through the five senses. These objects are all 'substances', understood as that which lacks internal relations to anything beyond themselves. Even the self is characterised in terms of substance. As soon as we orient our understanding around experience or subjectivity as the primary ground of our world of perceived objects, the classical approach is shattered. This is a radical proposal that involves both destruction of an unsatisfactory orthodoxy and reconstruction on a different foundation.

The shattering of the dominant tradition brings the subjective aspect of existence to the forefront where it belongs. I therefore pursue a philosophy of life which starts with human feelings and sees feeling in some form as present in all existence all the way down through animals and in attenuated form in cells and atoms and however much further one can go. This philosophy speaks of the feelings of God also. This philosophy is radical and controversial. It is not at all widely recognised. Its various names, panexperientialism, panpsychism and psychicalism, are meant to stand in strong contrast to materialism, mechanism or physicalism. It is the explicit viewpoint of so-called process thought or *constructive postmodernism* . This is to be contrasted with both *modernism* (or *mech-*

anism) and *deconstructive postmodernism* or *ultramodernism* (of the French antirationalists such as Derrida and Foucault) (Griffin et al. 1993). This latter view is postmodern in the sense that it carries the mechanistic (modern) worldview to its logical conclusion. It is deconstructive because it implies that anyone who thinks that some questions have right and wrong answers, which can be confirmed or refuted by evidence and argument, is a cretin. That academia should indulge in such frivolous game-playing is further discussed later in this chapter.

It is odd that at present the idea of mind as basic to nature as a whole is more acceptable to physicists than to biologists, as physicist Freeman Dyson (1988) says:

> The mind, I believe, exists in some very real sense in the universe. But is it primary or an accidental consequence of something else? The prevailing view among biologists seems to be that the mind arose accidentally out of molecules of DNA or something. I find that very unlikely. It seems more reasonable to think that mind was a primary part of nature from the beginning and we are simply manifestations of it at the present stage of history. It's not so much that mind has a life of its own as that the mind is inherent in the way the universe is built, and life is nature's way to give mind opportunities it wouldn't otherwise have. (p. 72)

Physicist Paul Davies (1992) also argues for the reality of mind at the heart of the universe. I return to this issue in subsequent chapters.

I have emphasised that what matters most for each of us are the feelings we have and that we engender. So why go any further and try to explain the basis of these experiences? Does it really matter what view we have of the nature and basis of our feelings? There is, I believe, a very practical answer to this question. It was put better than I can by quantum physicist David Bohm (1982), who warns us against the dangers of illusion and delusion in these matters:

> In the long run it is far more dangerous to adhere to illusion than to face what the actual fact is. And secondly, you can say, what is the point of life if you live in an invented world; if there is no

relationship either to the world or to the people or to anything? It isn't a relationship if you are related to something which is not there, or which is just there to make yourself feel comfortable. I think we all have this tendency and it is the problem of mankind. I could put it in terms of three words: illusion, delusion, and collusion. They are all based on the word *ludere*, meaning 'to play'. You can see illusion as playing false with perception, delusion as playing false with thought and collusion as people playing false together to support their illusions and delusions. This is the thing which has always made mankind's life miserable, and which is threatening our survival. We can't face the implications of what we're doing, and it will lead us over the edge, into the abyss (p. 362).

The thoughts we have about the world, about our feelings and our place in the world are crucially important for us and for the world. The implications of a basically false view will, as Bohm suggests, lead us over the edge, into the abyss. So it is, I shall claim, with the present dominant mechanistic view that rejects the reality of the subjective.

It is helpful initially to consider briefly how the proponents of the modern worldview came to suppose that there was something unreal about feelings and that the only real things are tables and planets and rocks and computers and all that we call objects or things. The reification (which means thingification) of the world goes back to the Greek atomists, and in particular Democritus and Lucretius two and a half millennia ago. They conceived the real world as being made of individual bits of stuff called atoms and nothing else. 'By convention there is sweet,' said Democritus, 'by convention there is bitterness, by convention hot and cold, by convention colour; but in reality there are only atoms and the void.' A. N. Whitehead (1978, p. 29) called this the doctrine of vacuous actuality. It is the doctrine of modern materialism.

Modernism (or materialism), as we know it today, stems from the sixteenth and seventeenth centuries. The Middle Ages immediately before that were dominated (in the Western world) by scholasticism, which depended upon such authorities as Aristotle, Augustine and Thomas Aquinas. There were other minority streams of thought such as alchemy, which had both scientific and magical aspects and were important in emphasising scientific experiment before the main renaissance of science in the sixteenth century.

The revolution of science in the sixteenth and seventeenth centuries with Copernicus, Galileo and Newton constituted a renaissance of science on a large scale. The real world became what science could investigate, which amounted to whatever could be weighed and measured. But these founders of modernism were dualists. They recognised two types of real things. There was matter on the one hand and mind and soul on the other hand. Only matter was subject to scientific analysis. These great scientists were the heirs of the atomists of the ancient world, for they conceived of bodies, be they stars or people, as composed exclusively of atoms of matter. The difference between different bodies was only in the arrangement, density and motion of these atoms. Qualities such as size, shape and mass are the only qualities to be considered really real, that is to say the qualities that are purely objective, quantitative and impersonal. Galileo, Descartes and Locke called these *primary* qualities.

However, our senses report the presence of other qualities, which seem to be in objects, such as colour, sound, smell, taste, heat and so on. These they called *secondary* qualities (today *qualia*). They were so called because, being irrelevant for the purposes of mechanics, they were thought not to be objective entities. In this view the rose is not really red. It is composed of atoms and nothing else. Thirdly are those aspects such as consciousness, purpose, emotions, and experiences of virtue and beauty that came to be called *tertiary* qualities. The dominance of this three-fold view, which was developed in the seventeenth century, brought the overthrow of scholasticism. But it had its problems. All the great scientists of this age were theists. They believed that God was real. But where did God fit into the scheme? They also had their problems with the nature of secondary and tertiary qualities and how the former related to really real matter.

The philosopher above all who tried to sort out these problems was Descartes. He said that if there is one thing he cannot doubt it is that he is an experiencing subject. So he accepted that he had a mind which was different from atoms. 'Let it be so,' he said; 'still it is at least quite certain that it seems to me that I see light, that I hear noise and that I feel heat. That cannot be false; properly speaking it is what is in me called feeling (*sentire*); and used in this precise sense that is no other thing than thinking' (Whitehead 1978, p. 41). Descartes leaves us in no doubt as to what he thinks is the reality of his feelings. However, his solution to explain the world was a completely dualistic one. There were material things and there were mental things (feelings) and they were complete opposites so it was hard to see how they could interact, though Descartes insisted that they did. He finally admitted (to Princess Christina) that he could not explain how mind and matter, being totally different, could interact. Each of them was a 'thing' in the sense that they were what he called substances. He tells us what he meant by *substance*: 'And when we conceive of *substance*, we merely conceive an existent thing which requires nothing but itself in order to exist' (Whitehead 1930, p. 92).

Descartes was not merely a dualist. He proposed three types of substance: bits of matter, minds and God. Other followers of Descartes, such as Malebranche, tried to explain the interaction between mind and matter by reference to God. The eventual demise of God led therefore to the demise of dualism. The resultant atheistic and materialistic view is what now passes for the *modern scientific worldview* or *modernism*. This was not the view of the founders of modern science in the seventeenth century (such as Newton, Boyle, Locke, Descartes and Mersenne). It was the view they wanted to avoid. It is today the presupposition of the dominant scientific worldview which excludes from its analysis secondary and tertiary qualities. It is one of my objectives to show that this view and practice are disastrous for any attempt to appreciate the nature of the world, despite the fact that this view is still dominant in science.

Bits of matter became the most real things in this modern worldview, with mind being an enigma. There were also those, such as Thomas Hobbes, who dropped God and minds, retaining only matter. Yet others, such as George Berkeley, retained God and minds but not matter. Still others dropped matter and minds, retaining God alone so that the temporal world became an appearance only.

A main point of such philosophies is that they presuppose individual substances 'which require nothing but itself in order to exist'. In *constructive postmodern philosophy* no such substances exist (Chapter 3).

The point of this brief bit of history is to indicate how easy it was for the scientific view of the world in the seventeenth century which was dualistic (as it included the reality of minds and souls) to become the *modern worldview* which regards stuff or atoms as the only real things. All could be reduced to matter and that is what science did. The science of substances was highly successful in dealing with the motion of steel balls on inclined planes and the movement of planets, but it did not attempt to deal with minds and feelings, nor for that matter with God. Nevertheless, this science transformed the world with its rejection of authority and superstition and its practice of observation and experiment. But there has been a price to pay for a worldview which has been unable to include feelings and the subjective aspects of existence that are so real in our experience. Despite being a useful heuristic tool for three centuries it has become a massive obstacle to the understanding of feelings and the secondary and tertiary qualities.

The scientific revolution, which began in the sixteenth century, was part of the Enlightenment which could be said to have started about the same time and reached its peak in the eighteenth century. The Enlightenment brought education, freedom from authority and an age of reason. But for all the good it brought, by the 1760s the scientific and philosophical speculation of the Enlightenment had reached an impasse. Hampson (1990) in his history of the Enlightenment says that by this time, 'Chance, or the blind determinism of matter in regular but aimless motion, appeared to regulate the operation of the universe and the destiny of man. If metaphysical speculation had any meaning at all — which the sceptics denied — it served merely to open a window on the blank wall of necessity.' (p. 186)

The objective and the subjective

The basic distinction that has to be made in this debate, which had a long history, is not primarily between mind and matter but between the objective and the subjective. I have some objective understanding of my cat. I know what it appears to me to be. But I do not know what my cat is in itself — what it is like to be that cat. That is the subjective aspect of my cat. What do I have direct knowledge of? Does my experience give me any knowledge of anything in itself? Yes — my experience in itself. My own consciousness is the one thing in all the universe I have direct knowledge of. Indeed, everything else, including my idea of my cat's feelings, is inferred. He may not be exactly as I see him. It is the external world of billiard balls and cats, not the internal one of my consciousness, that can only be inferred. To think otherwise (as do physicalists) is to put the cart before the horse. Our own private consciousness is the only thing each of us knows directly. We infer the rest.

It seems to me indubitable, when we reflect on our lives, that we do in fact experience the world in two quite different ways. I experience the world as a world of objects through my five senses. This is the world with which science has been concerned up to now. But I also experience life in non-sensory feelings as an inner awareness. Newton observed the fall of an apple and if he wished he could have measured objectively the speed of the fall and the mass of the apple. That was one aspect of what was going on. However, if Newton had a small daughter when he observed the fall of the apple, and if he had picked up the apple and given it to her, his report would have contained no reference to her delight in eating it, nor to what might have been his own enjoyment in watching her. It would have been possible to observe scientifically the outward expression of their enjoyment, but no such description of these would be the equivalent of what the experience meant to both of them. Yet it is just such subjective experiences that are the most substantial part of living.

We speak of a warm-hearted person as someone whose feeling and thinking work together in a harmonious way. When we think of Augustine or Nietzsche or Whitehead as impassioned thinkers, we mean that their lives have been dominated by attitudes in which rational insight together with intense feeling have reached a remarkable synthesis. This is the real nature of integrity, the root meaning of which is wholeness. For many of us our rational insights lead us in certain directions and our feelings in another. We are distracted by different interests and torn apart by divergent loyalties. There is no integrity between feeling and insight. So Hume correctly stated that intellect without passion is barren. A further discussion of this is given under the heading 'feeling and reason', later in this chapter.

Those who know the philosopher Charles Hartshorne are aware of his amazing capacity to bring out the meaning of a haphazard incident that arises during a taxi ride or on a casual walk through a city park. He can bring aspects of his philosophy to bear on the call of a bird or the brilliance of a flower. I vividly recall walking with him through the campus of the University of Sydney early one morning to listen to bird songs. When we came upon a flame tree, brilliant in the sunshine with its mass of scarlet flowers, more so because the leaves of spring had not yet arrived, he turned to me and said: 'Don't you think there is a quality in bright sunshine and brilliant flowers that we experience as something quite wonderful?' He was at that moment experiencing more than the objective world revealed by his five senses. And the songs of the birds which he was recording were more than wavelengths that could be put on tape. Indeed his chief interest in them was their aesthetic quality.

The feeling side of life is the subjective side. The description of the outward events of the falling apple and of the eating of the apple are the objective aspects. Both are real. The objective aspects become public information for anyone who wants to know about the fall of the apple. The subjective aspect of what the girl felt when she ate the apple is private information for her alone. The outsider can only guess at what these feelings are for her. It is in the network of internal relations we have with the world and with people that reality is most fully revealed.

A lot of our feelings are responses to data provided by the five senses. Between the red rose and my feelings of its redness are connecting links that have to do with photons in the light reflected from the rose hitting the photosensitive cells of the retina at the back of my eye. From there the signal is processed through four other layers of the retina and passes through the optic nerve to a part of the brain called the lateral geniculate nucleus. From there the signal goes to the striate cortex of the brain and then through the rest of the visual cortex. Eventually this complex electrochemical process causes a conscious visual experience. I see red.

These links are studied by physiologists who investigate the electrical impulses and the chemical changes involved. But in addition to all that information is the fact that I have a feeling of the quality redness. The feeling I have eludes the scientific analysis. It is the subjective side whereas the scientific analysis is the objective side of what is happening. Because the objective can be studied in detail with great accuracy it is easy to suppose that this is all that is involved. Indeed dominant schools of philosophy such as physicalism proclaim just that. An alternative proposition, which I find more realistic, is that both sides, the objective and the subjective, exist. They are the two sides of the one phenomenon.

If physicalism were true then one ought to be able to convey everything there is to know about what seeing or hearing is to one who has been blind or deaf from birth, simply by describing the whole physics and chemistry of seeing or hearing. But no matter how complete such a description may be, it will not convey to such a person what it is like to see or to hear. Or as has been said: 'If what I want when I drink fine wine is information about its chemical properties, why don't I just read the label?' (Dennett 1991, p. 383).

Likewise, suppose you say to me: 'I am in pain'. There are two sorts of facts that have to do with your statement. One is that you have unpleasant sensations. This is the subjective aspect of your pain. The other is that there is a series of physical and chemical links from pain receptors on your body through pathways of the nervous system to your brain. This is the objective side of pain, which the neurophysiologist studies. But no description of the objective physiological side of the pain enables me, the observer, to experience the subjective side, which is your feeling of pain.

If I said to you that your pain is *nothing but* the chemical events in your nerves, you would have good reason to tell me I didn't know what I was talking about. Someone who had a complete knowledge of the neurophysiology of pain would still not know what a pain is if he or she did not know what it felt like. The physical and chemical description of pain is not incorrect. It is incomplete. In more general terms the objective description does not give a complete account of what is happening because it omits the subjective aspect. For further discussion of this example, see Searle (1992, pp. 116-18).

The subjective experience of pain is itself influenced by the state of mind of the sufferer. In the Second World War, wounded front-line soldiers required less analgesia than did non-military surgical patients, even when their injuries were far more massive. This has been explained by considering the mental state of the wounded soldier and the non-military patient. Soldiers saw real benefit in being wounded, as they no longer faced risk on the battlefield. They focused on the better future, whereas surgical patients focused more on their present pain (Beecher 1956). Positive thoughts change the chemistry of the brain so the injured soldier who saw the benefits of being wounded suffered less pain that would otherwise have been the case.

But how do such thoughts influence the degree of pain? The neurophysiology of pain is complex. Nerve endings that cover the surface of the body send information about pain to the brain. What evidently happens is that cells in the injured region produce chemicals called prostaglandins that sensitise nerve endings in the skin, causing them to send messages to a special region in the spinal cord called the substantia gelatinosa. This region serves as a gateway for receiving or closing off pain messages from the injured region. This region also receives messages from the brain. Messages from the brain can turn off the information of pain coming to the spinal cord from the nerve endings at the injured site. This is the route by which thought can influence pain. The control is even more complex. Morphine-like chemicals called endomorphins are produced in the pituitary gland at the base of the brain in response to pain in the body. Endomorphins have receptors all over the brain and spinal cord. On being influenced by endomorphins, the receptors cause the brain and spinal cord to send messages to the pain gateway in the spinal cord to close the pain gateway (Gazzaniga 1988, pp. 29-33).

Many of our feelings are like this example of pain. They are mediated by one or other of the five senses. In the case of pain the sense is akin to touch, since it is nerve endings on the surface of the body that are the sensors. We know something of what it is like to see, taste, touch, hear and smell. But even our senses are limited. What would it be like to see with sonar as do bats, or to navigate along electromagnetic lines as do birds? We see colour and hear sounds only over a limited range of the spectrum of colour and sound. The colour range of sentience of a honey bee extends further into the ultraviolet end of the spectrum than does ours. Snakes can see into the infra-red end of the spectrum. Cats see only in black and white. Porpoises and some moths can hear beyond the range of sounds that we can hear. Dogs hear higher sound frequencies than we can.

Some physicalists, who recognise that subjective categories such as our feelings are different from purely objective categories used in physics and chemistry, try to devise a language to eliminate all subjective terms. David Armstrong says that we have 'general scientific grounds for thinking that man is nothing but a physical mechanism...that mental states are, in fact, nothing but physical states of the central nervous system', so that we should be able to 'give a complete account of man in purely physicochemical terms' (Armstrong 1979, pp. 67, 75). In a similar vein his fellow Australian philosopher John Smart (1979) says 'That everything should be explicable in terms of physics...except the occurrence of sensations seems to me to be frankly unbelievable' (p. 52).

These reductionist views, which had their modern birth in the seventeenth century, were already, in that century, being attacked by the Cambridge Platonist Ralph Cudworth who may have had Hobbes in mind when he wrote:

> For the atheist-materialist, mind is but a mere whiffling, evanid and fantastic thing; so that the most absolutely perfect of all things in the universe is grave, solid, and substantial senseless matter...A

modern atheistic pretender to wit hath publicly owned the same conclusion, that 'mind is nothing but local motion in the organic parts of a man's body'. These men have been sometimes indeed a little troubled with the fancy, apparition or seeming of cognition — that is, the consciousness of it, as knowing not what to make thereof...but they put it off again and satisfy themselves that the reality of cognition is nothing but local motion; as if there were not as much reality in fancy and consciousness as there is in local motion (Willey 1953, pp. 158-9).

A huge world of experience is available to us from our five senses. They are our windows to the external world. But what we observe is not a reflection of nature itself but a construction from data provided by the senses. Our brain sorts out these data and builds a picture of the world. Through vision and touch I do not know what a billiard ball is in itself but only know it as it appears to me. But observation is even more complex than this analysis suggests. Thought precedes observation. No one directs attention when there is nothing that he expects to see. Whitehead (1929, p. 73) points out that millions had seen apples fall from trees, but Newton had in his mind the mathematical relationship of forces between bodies. Millions had seen lamps swinging in churches, but Galileo had in his mind this same mathematical relationship. Millions had seen animals prey on each other, plants choking each other, millions had endured famine and thirst but Charles Darwin had in his mind the Malthusian relationship between the capacity of living organisms to increase in numbers and the limits of the environment in which they had to live. When he wrote up his journal of researches in South America he tells us that he never went into the jungle without having some hypothesis in mind. He didn't go there with a blank mind but with particular questions to ask of nature. If there is no scheme for observations to fit into, their significance is lost. It is claimed by some that some scientists have made discoveries by chance observations. Alexander Fleming is said to have discovered penicillin by the chance observation of a clear area surrounding colonies of micro-organisms on his cultures. But as Louis Pasteur said before Fleming's time, 'chance only favours the mind which is prepared'.

We don't see what is really there for these two reasons. On the one hand the mind is selective in its observations and, secondly, of those observations selected the mind makes its own constructions of what is there.

Normal minds see the world as well-organised. We can filter out what is important and meaningful from the buzzing flood of sensory information. But this filtering process may go wrong. One theory of schizophrenia is that, instead of the brain filtering out information, every sensation seems to crush in at once. Consciousness dissolves into a chaotic clamour that may last for days or even weeks (Torrey et al., 1993).

Love and the sensationalist fallacy

Are the five senses our only access to the world around us? To suppose that all knowledge of the real world comes to us through the five senses alone is the 'sensationalist fallacy'. What about our intuitive experiences of anticipation, hope, love, and what some people call religious experiences? These experiences are real enough to those who have them. There is an objective aspect of these feelings, too, that can be studied. But this is a more difficult scientific exploration than that of the five senses. From that perspective we ask in this section — what is romantic love? And in the next section we ask — what is depression? These are two deep feelings that most people can identify with.

In romantic love, information from the senses and the non-sentient are mixed together. Lovers claim they feel as if they were being swept away. They have an intensity of feeling that blots out pretty well everything else. Tim is 40 years old, married contentedly, successful in business, and a good family man. Yet at this late stage he has fallen in love with another woman. He is having trouble sleeping. After all these years he finds he cannot tolerate the sound of his wife's regular breathing. At three in the morning he slips out of bed, walks the garden and may leave the house in his car. Back home he climbs into the bed. His wife enquires if something is the matter. Telephones become both a torture and something that is irresistible. He is constantly dialling his loved one's number. He waits for the first ring, imagines her hearing it in her apartment and then hangs up. Time and again he has driven to her apartment, just to see if her car is there. When it was not he drove a block away and waited until he saw her car round the bend. He has no idea what he would say to her if she saw him and stopped. He would be petrified. All he needs right then is a brief glimpse and to know that she is all right.

He has spoken to her on other occasions that seemed to him more natural. She suggests they just be friends. But he says to himself he has enough friends already. Another friend is not what he wants. What does he want? He is not at all sure. For that matter he is not exactly sure what he sees in this woman. He does not know very much about her. He even has the fleeting feeling that if he does get to know her he will find out something dreadful. That could stop it all. But nothing stops the feeling he has for her. He turns on the radio and hears the Cole Porter tune 'I Get a Kick Out of You.' That's it. But why oh why? He longs for some sort of equanimity to his life these days. But none comes, only the sight of her. He has lost interest in food. His friends enquire about his health. 'Falling in love', says one of his closest friends, 'is crazy as hell'. 'Just tell me', he says, 'how I can make it stop'.

Dorothy Tennov (1979) wrote *Love and Limerence* about this feeling. Limerence is her term for the phenomenon that Tim is experiencing. The preface to her book is irresistible, so much so that I quote it in full, except for the final sentence:

I want you.

I want you forever, now, yesterday, and always. Above all, I want you to want me.

No matter where I am or what I am doing, I am not safe from your spell. At any moment, the image of your face smiling at me, of your voice telling me you care, or of your hand in mine, may suddenly fill my consciousness, rudely pushing out all else.

The expression 'thinking of you' fails to convey either the quality or quantity of this unwilled mental activity. 'Obsessed' comes closer but leaves out the aching. A child is obsessed on Christmas Eve. But it's a happy prepossession full of excitement, curiosity, and expectation. *This* prepossession is an emotional roller-coaster that carries me from the peak of ecstasy to the depths of despair. And back again.

I bear the thought of other topics when I must, but prolonged concentration on any other subject is difficult to tolerate. I must admit that it has happened on occasion that some entertainment or distraction overwhelmed thought of you, and I was suddenly freed from my pain and for an instant viewed you from a new perspective. I don't seek distractions. I'm too afraid that they won't distract after all and I'll be imprisoned somewhere saying polite nothings while I long to give myself up to desiring you with all my passions; to Tin Pan Alley's 'burning desire'.

Everything reminds me of you. I try to read, but four times on a single page some word begins the lightning chain of associations that summons my mind away from my work, and I must struggle to return my attention to the task at hand. Often I give up easily, leave my desk, and throw myself down on my bed, where my body lies still while my imagination constructs long and involved and plausible reasons to believe that you love me.

Or I remember. After the weekend in Vermont my brain replayed each moment. Over and over. You said you loved me, at dusk by the waterfall. Ten thousand reverberations of the scene sprinkled my successive days with happiness. Remember the state, do you? (pp. vii-viii).

Being in love is both ecstasy and pain. The Maya understand the pangs of love, for the word *yaii* means both love and pain. The lover's pain has been called love's affliction or lovesickness. It is the feeling that ensues when a lover is separated, however briefly, and languishes and pines for the beloved. That it is timeless is borne out by Vita Sackville-West (1992) in a letter from her seventeenth-century ancestor, which she quotes:

I am in pain till I can clear some doubts that have kept me waking all night; something I observed in your looks which shewed you had been displeased, at what I dare not ask; but till I know I must suffer the torment of uncertain guessing; though I am pretty well assured I could not be concerned in it... being so perfectly yours, that it will of necessity be counted your own fault if ever I offend you, since 'tis you alone have the government of all my actions but of my very thoughts, to confirm you in the belief of this truth I do from this moment give up to you all my pretences to freedom or any power over myself, and though you may justly think it below you to be owned the sovereign of so mean a dominion as my heart, I have yet confidence upon my knees to offer it to you; since never any prince could boast of so clear a title, and so absolute power, as you shall ever possess in it (p. 35).

Francesco Petrarch, the Italian poet of love, wrote some 400 love poems over a period of 21 years in the fourteenth century. The poems were addressed to his Platonic mistress Laura, from the day they met to her tragic death, probably from the black death. Petrarch's love for Laura was unrequited and swung from delirious desire into the depths of despair. For these 21 years Petrarch was lovesick for Laura. Lovesickness leads to a 'broken heart' when one of the partners leaves and rejects the call of the lovesick one for reunion. Lovelorn suffering is intense and akin to the grief of bereavement. Francesco Petrarch knew it all.

Being 'in love' is an example of an intense feeling, a subjective state of particular internal relations that is of overwhelming importance to the person in love. One's feelings then are all that matters. Rationality gets thrown to the wind. More generally, whatever state of mind I happen to be in, what matters most is always my feeling. That is reality for me at the time.

When Dorothy Tennov wrote her book she had virtually nothing to say about the objective side of limerence. At that time little was known. Just as there is an objective side that science can study of the phenomenon of seeing a red rose or feeling pain, so there is an objective side of falling in love. Love is also chemistry. This fact does not in any sense deny the reality of the feeling of euphoria.

The euphoria of falling in love is associated with a variety of chemicals that are secreted into the bloodstream from the brain. They include dopamine, norepinephrine and especially the amphetamine-like substance phenylethylamine (PEA). PEA gives you that silly smile that you flash at strangers, says Anthony Walsh (1991). When we meet someone who is attractive to us or anticipate seeing our lover, 'the whistle blows at the PEA factory' says Walsh, and we get another fix. PEA is said to give love's special kick. Sooner or later the kick it gives peters out. But another set of chemicals seems to take over in enduring love. These are opiates called endomorphins and are produced in the brain. They are nature's pain-killers, producing a soothing effect. When a lover is abandoned the absence of endomorphins results in the opposite feeling of despondency and mental pain which poets call a 'broken heart'. The lover suffers withdrawal symptoms. The full story, as at present understood, is more complicated than this, as Walsh (1991) and Gazzaniga (1988) show. Suffice, at this stage, to say that the knowledge that there is a biochemical background to the state of being in love illustrates the close relation between our feelings and our physical or chemical state. It does not imply that one is more real than the other. Feelings are real and chemicals are real. What sets off the chain of chemical reactions varies. It might be the sight of a face, the touch, smell or the thought of a face or even the thought of a touch.

Sexual arousal is an aspect of passionate love. The usual environmental circumstances that lead to it are well known. What is less well known is that some circumstances that in themselves have nothing to do with sexual arousal can predispose a person to arousal. In an experiment, men had to cross one of two bridges in Vancouver. One was a 150-metre-long, two-metre-wide bridge that swung and swayed over a gorge with a 75-metre drop. The other was a stable, solid bridge upstream from the other. Meeting the men at the other end of each bridge was a woman who maintained she needed a questionnaire filled out for a class project. She said she didn't have time then to explain the project in detail and gave her phone number. Guess who called? Only the men from the bridge that swung and swayed. The somewhat frightening experience predisposed these men to pursue the attractive woman who met them at the end of the bridge (Gazzaniga 1988, p. 172).

Sexual arousal may be an aspect of religious ecstasy if we are to take Bernini's depiction of the ecstasy of St Teresa seriously. In the Cornaro chapel in Santa Maria della Vittoria in Rome is Bernini's wondrous sculpture of the ecstasy of St Teresa. He illustrates exactly the passage in the saint's life in which she describes the supreme moment of her life: how an angel with a flaming golden arrow pierced her heart repeatedly, 'The pain was so great that I screamed aloud, but simultaneously felt such infinite sweetness that I wished the pain to last eternally. It was the sweetest caressing of the soul by God' (Clark 1969, p. 191). A Frenchman said on observing this deeply moving work of art: 'If that's divine love I've had it too!'.

Depression

An analysis analogous to the understanding of the euphoria of falling in love can be made of the opposite end of the feeling spectrum, such as the feeling of depression. Mental pain such as depression is just as real as the pain of migraine or kidney colic. However, the basic causes of depression are largely unknown. The precise role of chemicals is hypothetical and not yet proven in any rigorous way. The role of anti-depressant drugs is to put into the body chemicals that block the action of chemicals involved in the depressed or anxious state. A number of drugs that increase the concentration of chemicals involved in the transmission of impulses within the nervous system are often effective in the treatment of depressive symptoms. Accounts of what is known of the complex chemistry of depression can be found in Gazzaniga (1988, Chapter 6), Sapolsky (1994, Chapter 11) and Nuland (1994).

There are two main sorts of triggers of depression. One sort is precipitated by sudden changes within the chemistry of the brain. This is known as endogenous depression. Another sort is precipitated by surrounding personal conditions such as grief. This is called exogenous depression. These triggers set off changes in chemicals in the brain.

One theory of addiction to drugs and alcohol is that drug dependency is caused when a sober life lacks stimulation and meaning for a person who then becomes joyless and depressed. There is evidence that religion that gives a sense of meaning and purpose to life can be highly therapeutic for the drug dependent person. 'Drug abuse is not a problem with drugs, it's a problem with pleasure' said Dr Roy Mathews of the Duke University Medical Center for alcoholism and addiction. He refers to dopamine, a chemical produced in the brain, that acts on the nervous system to create sensations of well-being and euphoria. He suggests that the high that comes from some religious activities may have a similar chemical effect. Religious groups have had success in breaking addictions, such as those of opium field workers in Buddhist Thailand and Muslim Pakistan. Members of Alcoholics Anonymous practise successfully a therapy which has a 12-step program that stresses spiritual dependence upon a power beyond themselves. The new meaning they find in their lives displaces the need for alcohol (Witham 1995).

The point I want to make is that depression, as with other feelings, has its subjective aspects which are the feelings of depression and its objective aspect which is the changed chemistry in the brain in the depressed state. As we discover more about the relation between the two the more likely we shall be able to control these unhappy and related states.

Psychoneuroimmunology

Depression, along with other states such as chronic stress, have an effect on the activity of cells and chemicals that are responsible for our immunity to foreign invaders such as bacteria. Depression and stress can cause a suppression of the immune system. This is an example of what is called psychoneuroimmunology. It is a study that investigates the relation between how we feel and think about ourselves and our relations with others, on the one hand, and disease, on the other hand. Depression, loneliness, bereavement, anxiety and other life-stresses can cause a depression of the immune system leaving us susceptible to a variety of diseases. Upper respiratory tract infections were more severe in a group of depressed, stressed carers than in a control group. There is evidence suggesting that alleviating depression and stress makes a difference to the progression of skin cancer, breast cancer and cancers of the blood and bone marrow. Patients with leukaemias and lymphomas were found to live significantly longer when they received regular supportive home visits. In another study of women with breast cancer, those who received group therapy as well as standard cancer therapy survived twice as long on average as those who had standard therapy alone (Walsh 1991, p. 109; Sapolsky 1994, Chapter 8; Mestel 1994).

Most studies on the relation of mental states to the immune system have been on the effect of stress. For example, university students during exam times had depressed immune responses which were indicated by changes in cells involved in immunity such as T cells and reduced levels of gamma-interferon which is a protein that stimulates immune responses. By contrast, medical students examined after a summer vacation had healthy immune responses. It is also known that elderly people caring for partners who have Alzheimer's disease are affected like the medical students under the stress of exams (Mestel 1994).

What all this means is that it does really matter to our health how we feel. The big question remains as to how the subjective state of the brain communicates to the immune system in the rest of our bodies. That is an area of active research at present.

Other feelings

So one could continue to identify different feelings in the total spectrum of feeling and the associated biochemistry. For example, somewhere between the extremes of euphoria of love and the depths of depression is compassion. Compassion is a feeling as real as the passion of being in love or being anxious but, so far as I am aware, less is known of its objective side. The word is derived from the Latin *cum* and *patior*, meaning 'to suffer with.' We normally speak of extending compassion to one who is suffering in some way. However, its fuller meaning is extended to include experiencing another's feelings through empathic identification, be it with another's joy or grief.

The aspect of compassion as an internal relation between one person and another becomes evident when we consider the outward behaviour of two visitors to a patient in hospital. The first visitor may bring flowers, give a greeting, start a cheerful conversation, offer a drink and hold hands. Yet compassion may be wholly absent. The second may do all these things. She looks into the eyes of the patient, stretches out her hand, and truly sees the suffering of her friend. She, in some way, experiences her friend's suffering, and tears come to her eyes. They are her friend's tears. She has begun to see the world through the eyes of her friend. Through compassion, she shares another's suffering. C. S. Lewis, as depicted in the play and film *Shadowland*, felt such depth of compassion for his wife Joy in her final illness and suffering that he says he felt her experience of pain. He wondered if he was, in fact, taking some of her pain away from her.

Our existence is more than a succession of bare facts. It is rather a succession of different layers of feeling, of zest after purposes, of joy and grief, of interest concentrated on self, of interest directed beyond self, of life-weariness and life-zest, of ascent up high peaks and descent into the abyss. None of our feelings need be end-states. The head, however bloodied, and the heart, however broken, may win through the struggles of life and put back into life spiritual values that were not there before. If something terrible happens to you, you can either become heroic in the face of the awfulness of it and end up a stronger person or become diminished by it, become a victim and give in to self-pity and rage.

Our state of mental well-being is greatly dependent upon our relations of compassion with others. A student from a broken home who is full of life and zest tells me that he was saved by his grandmother. Another student tells me it was an aunt who helped him through times of great stress. We depend very much on the bonds of compassion we establish with others. The father of the prodigal son 'had compassion'. The Samaritan 'showed compassion'.

To live apathetically from moment to moment amid the abundance, is to deprive oneself. The narrowness of our participating sense of value makes us poor. It is because of our prejudice and blindness that we do not see the abundance in the midst of which we stand. To be open to the values that press in on us from moment to moment is to win greatness from life. For whoever lives with this attitude, every restriction of experience is recognised as superficiality, dullness, barrenness, a waste of life and, when it degenerates into a pose, as an unworthy renunciation, pessimism and ingratitude.

That most practical of economists John Maynard Keynes said in his book *The General Theory of Employment Interest and Money* that 'ideas are more powerful than is generally understood. Indeed the world is ruled by little else. The power of vested interest is vastly exaggerated compared with the gradual encroachment of ideas.'

Deconstructive postmodernists, such as Foucault and Derrida, pour scorn on the values that make for fullness of life. What they deconstruct or eliminate are the ingredients necessary for a worldview through an antiworldview that gets rid of self, purpose, meaning and God. As Gertrude Himmelfarb (1994) argues in her devastating and responsible critique of them, and of those who find it fashionable to follow, they are at best frivolous game-players who make a virtue of their moral irresponsibility. At worst, they are set on destroying the standards that not only make their own activity possible but that also enable society to survive at all. Either way they are bad news. This is brilliantly portrayed by David Williamson's play *Dead White Males*. Williamson exposes the frivolity of this game in which the traditional values of the Western intellectual world are no longer regarded as the expression of universal values, but are simply the out-of-date ideology of the dead white males of the Eurocentric capitalist patriarchy.

Non-sensory feelings

The sensationalist fallacy is the assumption that the only source of our avenues of communication with the external world are the five sense organs. It is true that all exact scientific observation is derived from the data of the sense organs. However, the stimuli moulding most of our experiences are manifold. Besides the five senses, another kind of perception is going on. Romantic love, already discussed, is an example. The most compelling example of non-sensory perception is our knowledge and feeling of our own immediate past of a tenth or half a second ago. It is the foundation of one's immediate present experience, which is engaged in modifying it and adjusting it to other values and other purposes (Whitehead 1942, p. 211).

Memory is relating us unconsciously to thousands of incidents in the past. At any age of our life, we are every age we have been. This may be the case in certain sorts of panic attack which relate to particular childhood experiences. There is a long-running controversy among neurophysiologists about whether memory is located or distributed in the brain. Debate today is on how much is localised and how much is distributed.

In addition to memory, our present moment of experience has an anticipatory element reaching forward to the future. The purposes we envisage and the goals we set ourselves make strong inputs into our total experience of being alive. As Whitehead (1929) said: 'The conduct of human affairs is entirely dominated by our recognition of foresight determining purposes, and purpose issuing in conduct. Almost every sentence we utter and every judgment we form, presuppose our unfailing experience of this element of life' (p. 13).

All the multiplicity of influences from the past and the present and toward the future produces a single unitary experience right now for us. The chain of events are many. Billions or even trillions of cells in our brain seem to be linked together to produce our unitary experience, a feeling-emotional-intellectual-whole, the experience.

The term extrasensory perception (ESP) refers to the apparent gaining of information by telepathy, precognition and clairvoyance. The scientific community as a whole is pretty sceptical about the reality of such phenomena for two reasons. One is that for many the evidence is not compelling. The other reason is that ESP cannot be understood within the framework of traditional science. It is reasonable at this stage to keep an open mind on the subject.

Unconscious feelings

Goethe wrote: 'man cannot persist long in a conscious state, he must throw himself back into the unconscious for his root lives there' (Holroyd 1989, p. 146). To speak of feelings that are unconscious might seem to be a confusion in terms. This would indeed be the case if all feelings were conscious. However, I have argued for the use of the word feeling for the subjective element, whether it be conscious or not. In the case of human beings there is clinical and experimental evidence for the influence of the unconscious on a person's thoughts and actions. Hypnosis, subliminal perception and the response of patients to psychoanalytical questioning each provide evidence of the unconscious. Many of the activities involved in our controlled movements, such as walking or drinking a cup of tea, are unconscious. It is likely too that most of the information processing in the brain is unconscious (Kihlstrom 1993).

When Goethe spoke of our roots living in the unconscious he seems to have been referring to the unconscious mind that stores up experiences that may or may not come to light in the conscious mind. This concept has had an evolution since about 1750. However, Sigmund Freud on his seventieth birthday in 1926 remarked: 'The poets and philosophers before me discovered the unconscious; what I discovered was the scientific method by which the unconscious can be studied'. Well, not quite. Freud's work on dreams as a way into the unconscious has been amply corroborated, but his method had little in common with science.

Freud argued that the inference that the unconscious mind exists is analogous to the everyday inference for the existence of minds in other persons. We attribute minds to others because their behaviour justifies the inference. That inference relates also to our own behaviour when it warrants the ascription of intentions of which we are consciously unaware. Most of the activity of our mind is unconscious. Consciousness is merely the tip of the iceberg of our feelings. Most of our memories are such that we are not conscious of them at every moment. I can recall a lot of things that happened to me long ago in my youth but I bring them to consciousness only when the rare occasion warrants. A modern day concern which has led to court cases is how to distinguish a real experience of the past that becomes conscious in the present from fabrications of the past. Under therapy a person may claim to recall being abused as a child many years ago. But was that person really abused as a child? A court should require more evidence than the statement of the person who claims to have been abused a long way back in the past. Such evidence is usually not easy to get.

To Freud we owe the understanding of repression and of the many ways in which thoughts and feelings may surface from the unconscious as determinants of behaviour and attitudes. Freud said that the purpose of psychotherapy was to make the unconscious conscious. A man's attitude to his wife may be unconsciously determined by his attitude to his mother, perhaps leading to his expectation that his wife will be a mother to him. A woman at a critical period of her marriage said of her husband: 'He loved what he wanted me to be...I wasn't.' Textbooks of psychology are full of similar examples of deeply held unconscious concepts from early in life that can have a profound influence later on. In hypnosis some of these unconscious memories can be brought into consciousness.

A much-studied example of the unconscious mind is the phenomenon of multiple personality (Braude 1991). A person may have several different and relatively autonomous personalities. But at any one time only one of them is conscious for the person with this disorder. This phenomenon is sufficiently common to have justified the formation of the International Society for the Study of Multiple Personality and Dissociation with a membership of about 2000 (Braude 1991, p. 37).

Feelings in solitude and in a group

Much of the motivation of life comes through non-sensory feelings which might be experienced in solitude or, by contrast, in a group. Profound feelings come to us in solitude where there is little distraction from the five senses. We are alone with ourselves. Theoretical physicist Richard Feynman was in the habit of using a flotation tank in which he would float in the dark to cut out sensory feelings as much as possible, to be alone and undisturbed with his non-sensory feelings, preparing for the next lot of momentous ideas to build into his developing theories. Jesus went into the desert alone for 40 days, there to face in aloneness the inevitability of the future he had chosen. He was communicating with something beyond himself which produced profound feelings as well as insights. People who today practise meditation have to learn how to be alone.

Others discover profound feelings in community. Jesus gathered around him a small group of disciples. We are told in the records more about what happened to the disciples than to Jesus by being a member of a group. But presumably the inner relationships were mutual to both him and the disciples. The feelings of each got across to the others. Wieman (1947, pp. 39-40) identified four internal changes that happened to them.

First, the atomic exclusiveness of the disciples was broken so that they became freely receptive and responsive to the needs and aspirations of each other.

Second, each developed a greater sense of the meaning of their lives, a capacity to understand, to appreciate, to act with insight and power.

Third, their appreciable world expanded since they could now see through the eyes of others, feel their sensitivities and discern the secrets of many hearts. Those around them, who were initially seen as enemies, became neighbours to be shown compassion.

Fourth, in consequence of this they experienced a greater depth and breadth of community within their own group and eventually with a much wider world.

Most extraordinary of all was what happened after the death of Jesus to the creative power which this group of people experienced and which dominated their lives. It was neither diminished nor destroyed. Rather it was released from constraints and limitations previously confining it. The fellowship developed an organisation, rituals, symbols and documents by which the creative event that happened to a small group became perpetuated through other lands and through history.

What really happened to a bunch of simple fisherfolk and their friends was a mighty transformation of their inner lives of feeling that flooded them with an overwhelming purpose and will which became reflected in their outward lives of action. They discovered a richness of experience that was not there before. It brought a twofold gift of zest and harmony into their lives. Thinking back, each one must have felt how much he had missed before he became part of a group with its one overriding purpose.

To live apathetically from moment to moment amid the abundance of possibilities is nothing short of evil. The narrowness of our participation in the values or feelings of life makes us poor within. According to the gospel of Thomas, Jesus said: 'If you bring forth what is within you, what you bring forth will save you. If you do not bring forth what is within you, what you do not bring forth will destroy you'.

Our chief problems lie in the realm of our feelings or passions. Only a higher passion can quench the lower. Only the expulsive power of pure affection can exorcise a sordid lust. We are saved from fire by fire. As was said by Kierkegaard: 'No heart is pure that is not passionate, no virtue is safe that is not enthusiastic'. Purity of heart is to will one thing. That is the meaning of *enthusiasm*, which literally means *God within*.

Feeling and reason

Hume correctly said that intellect without passion is barren. We speak of a warm-hearted person as someone whose feeling and thinking work together in a harmonious way. When we think of Augustine or Nietzsche or Whitehead as impassioned thinkers, we mean that their lives were dominated by attitudes in which rational insight together with intense feeling have reached a remarkable synthesis. This is the real nature of integrity, the root meaning of which is wholeness. For many of us our rational insights lead us in certain directions and our feelings in another. We are distracted by different interests and torn apart by divergent loyalties. There is no integrity between feeling and reason.

The neurophysiologist Antonio Damasio (1994) makes a strong case that humanity is not suffering from a deficit of reasoning, but rather from a deficit in the emotions (feelings) that inform reason. He starts his book with an account of the history of Phineus Gage, a construction worker. In 1848 a heavy iron bar was dynamited through his left cheek, travelling up through the front of his brain and coming out through the top of his skull. Gage not only survived this freak accident but at first appeared to have all his faculties intact. It was only later that it became apparent that his personality had subtly changed. He could rationally decide what to do but he no longer seemed to care about the out-come. The emotions that normal people associate with various happenings were not there any more.

Demasio describes other people, patients of his, who also had damage to the frontal lobes of the brain similar to that experienced by Gage and who had shown the same inability to care about what happened to them. These people had lost their ability to make rational decisions along with the ability to process emotion normally. Their instrument of rationality could still be recruited; they still had access to the knowledge of the world in which to operate and the ability to tackle the logic of a problem remained intact. Yet many of their personal and social decisions were irrational. And, more often than not, they were disadvantageous to the individual and to others. It seems that their processes of reasoning were no longer affected by the weights that should have been imparted by emotion. Damasio used his knowledge of these people, whose brains had been damaged, to formulate his proposition that in normal people rational decision-making is guided by their emotions or feelings about the problem. What the brain decides is influenced by these feelings. In people with the sort of damage to the brain that Damasio studied, this connection between feeling and reason is broken down.

Damasio is critical of neuro-science's obsession with cognition (reasoning) as the defining feature of the function of the brain. Emotion, he insists, is equally important, if not more so. Computers are cognition machines, which is why they can play chess as well as humans, or even better (see Chapter 4). But humans bring emotions to bear on cognition. Damasio even pinpoints a region of the brain resonsible for integrating emotional responses with cognitive ones. He believes it lies somewhere in the frontal lobes of the brain. If Descartes said 'I think therefore I am' he was mistaken. If instead he said, as seems more likely, 'I feel therefore I am' he would have been closer to the mark. Damasio thinks he would have done even better had he said 'I am, therefore I emote and thus can interpret thought, predict consequences of action and make effective choices.'

When we fail to make the normal connection between feeling

and reason it is easy not to notice that our purported rational decisions are subtly manipulated by the emotions. It is easier not to be concerned about the possible negative consequences of the vicarious emotional experiences of violence as entertainment. It is easier to overlook the positive effect that well-tuned emotions can have in the management of human affairs. Damasio quotes Pascal, who prefigured this idea in the seventeenth century: 'It is on this knowledge of the heart and of the instincts that reason must establish itself and create the foundation for all its discourse'. We are only beginning now to uncover the relevant facts from neurobiology behind Pascal's profound insight.

The feeling of feeling

It is one thing to accept the reality of feelings in addition to the reality of the objective aspects that science investigates. But we need to go further than that. When I look at a rose and have the feeling of redness, the first impact of the rose on me is on the cells of the retina at the back of my eye which are sensitive to colours. When cells of the retina are hit by the light rays from the rose we presume that the particular wavelength causes chemical changes in the cells such that a particular message about redness is conveyed along the optic nerve to the sight centre of the brain. But is that all? Why can't we talk about the cells of the retina also having feelings? Physiologists never do. Yet there is as much reason for supposing that as for concluding that our brain has feelings. Nerve impulses to the brain don't just miraculously become converted from electricity into feelings. In some way they must register the feelings of the cells of the retina. Why not? There is no reason for excluding this possibility. Each cell is a well-integrated organism. Of course we don't suppose that the retinal cells have the feeling of redness that our brain gives us. But if they are sentient in some sense, then they have their own subjective response to the light waves hitting them. So we can say, with Whitehead and Hartshorne, that our feeling is the 'feeling of feeling' (in this case of our retinal cells) (Hartshorne 1987, p. 25).

In a similar way I could argue that when I am hit with a stone that bruises my muscles and I feel pain, my muscle cells themselves have some sort of feeling. It would not be correct to say that they have the pain that I feel, for my pain is compounded with messages from pain receptors in the muscles to centres in the brain that integrate into a unified experience of the messages from the muscle cells. Damage my cells and you hurt my cells and you hurt me. I participate in their feelings. Hartshorne (1987) calls this the social structure of experience and reality. He goes so far as to say:

> With the one three-word phrase, 'feeling of feeling' as he used it...Whitehead inaugurated a new epoch in the intellectual history of mankind. That it has been left for me to say this in so many words is a sign of how novel this usage was (p. 25).

In this way of looking at feelings we can say that all experiencing is 'feeling of feeling'. Memory is feeling of past feelings. Anticipation is feeling of feelings not yet concretely real in our experience.

Conclusion

Our feelings are the most important aspect of our life. When there is no feeling life has lost its value. Feelings are as real as atoms, tables and chairs.

It matters how we interpret our feelings in terms of a worldview or philosophy of life.

There is an objective and a subjective side to feelings. Love is also chemistry. So too are depression, stress and anxiety.

Feelings are both sensory and non-sensory.

Reason is based on feeling. When through accident, or in some other way, the capacity for feeling is destroyed, the rational aspect of life becomes irrational and such people become destructive to society. In a less dramatic way, all of us are subject to failing to make a creative connection between the feeling side of life and reason and then exhibit varying degrees of irrationality.

Feeling is feeling of feeling. This principle turns physicalist reductionism on its end. The proposition is that all objects and all subjects are ultimately reducible to feelings, despite the fact that there are aggregates of such objects, such as tables and rocks, that do not themselves feel (see Chapter 3).

2

Feelings of Animals

There is every gradation of transition between animals and men. In animals we can see emotional feeling, dominantly derived from bodily functions, and yet tinged with purposes, hopes, and expression.

A. N. WHITEHEAD (1966, p. 27)

In Chapter 1 we were concerned with the importance of feelings in humans, the great diversity of human feelings and how they point toward a much more feeling universe than we tend to allow. The emphasis of this chapter on non-humans is different. We need to establish first whether or not animals have feelings. I am pretty sure that if you ask your friends whether they think that cats and dogs and canaries have feelings they would say yes. Some of them would be prepared to guess that all animals have some sort of feelings. They might give as their reasons the same ones they would give for supposing that all humans have feelings. So why bother asking the question? One reason is that down the ages there has been variety of ideas about whether or not animals have feelings. Indeed, as we shall see, philosophers such as Descartes and theologians such as Malebranche argued that only humans have feelings. There are those today, as we shall see, who follow suit.

A second reason for asking the question — do animals have feelings? — is the practical consequence of denying feelings to animals. It has led to great cruelty. Today enormous numbers of people are, through modern technology, having a deleterious impact on the Earth's environment. One consequence of this is that animals are suffering more than ever. Each day many species become extinct. In the city of Beijing authorities decided that there is not enough food for humans and dogs and, moreover, that dogs cause a mess in the streets. So dogs have to go. The ownership of dogs is illegal. According to Elizabeth Thomas (1994) enforcing the law are Dog Police who go into homes where a dog is suspected. When they find one, it is crammed into a canvas bag and in front of the owners and neighbours they club the dog to death.

Most of us in the West do not see ourselves as participants in such brutality. However, we come close. The greatest slaughter of any wild mammal in the world is the millions of kangaroos shot every year in Australia because they are regarded as pests by farmers. In 1993 the quota for killing kangaroos was 5 million. Not far behind is the annual slaughter of Australian wild ducks in the annual open season for hunters. In both cases there is much cruelty to defenceless animals. And because of the growing demand of the world for meat, the way in which we get that meat is coming under closer scrutiny. Mass production of cattle and sheep leads to more, not less, cruelty.

The biologist J. B. S. Haldane, who had a more philosophical approach than most of his colleagues, said: 'For a scientific man a philosophy is not a creed but a programme'. The program which a philosophy about the feelings of animals suggests is that we be moved to care more for our fellow inhabitants of the Earth. The first step in caring is to become more sensitive to the feelings of animals. The second step is to begin to think about rights for animals, analogous to the way in which we think about human rights. These two propositions seem innocent enough, but to really take heed of them would be to start a revolution in both our thinking and our actions about animals.

The denial of consciousness or subjectivity in animals, by many psychologists and philosophers, has a history which hopefully might come to be seen as an historical aberration

In 1637 Descartes pronounced that non-human animals were like machines. He compared animals to the mechanisms of clocks, though somewhat more complicated. The human body was a machine also, but it had attached to it a mind which was a radically different kind of entity. Because Descartes knew he had feelings he knew he existed. Because humans have minds as well as bodies they are capable of having thoughts and feelings. But mere animals are different, said Descartes. He identified consciousness so completely with reason as to conclude that because animals do not reason they cannot be conscious at all. They are bodies without minds and therefore without thoughts and therefore without feelings. Hence his conclusion that animals do not feel pain, for pain is experienced only by beings capable of understanding their bodily sensations. Descartes believed that this view of animals absolved human beings from the suspicion of crime when they ate animals. It was a view gladly received by at least one physiological laboratory in France, of which Nicolas Fontaine wrote in 1738:

> They said the animals were clocks; that the cries they emitted
> when struck were only the noise of a little spring that had been

touched, but that the whole body was without feeling...they made fun of those who pitied the creatures as if they felt pain (Rachels 1990, p. 130).

Nicholas Malebranche, a contemporary of Descartes, welcomed this machine view of animals for another reason. The suffering of animals presented a serious theological problem for him and for others. The suffering of humans they explained as a consequence of the sin of Adam, which was transmitted by inheritance to the rest of the human race. But animals are not descended from Adam and so have no share in original sin. Descartes' view that animals have no feelings, and therefore do not suffer, exonerated God from any blame that might otherwise be laid against him (Rachels 1990, p. 130). Malebranche maintained with Descartes that animals cry but have no pain, they desire nothing, fear nothing and know nothing. This view was still current at the time Darwin published *The Origin of Species* in 1859, though Darwin was himself quick to repudiate such a view, as we shall see.

The main legacy of Descartes' view of animals as machines is not that it led a lot of people to believe that animals have no feelings. It probably didn't. Rather it cemented a view in the minds of natural scientists, and in that of many social scientists, that the world and all that is in it, including living creatures, are to be understood as if they were machines. The next step, which many took, was to say that animals are machines. That is a very different proposition.

An imprimatur for the mechanistic view of nature was given in 1859 by Darwin in *The Origin of Species*, which is a thoroughly mechanical explanation of evolution, despite the fact that Darwin did not accept the proposition that animals have no feelings. He saw them as much more like us. Indeed, he wrote a book in 1872 on *The Expression of the Emotions in Man and Animals,* in which he emphasised the similarities between humans and other animals. Darwin said that we underestimate the richness of the mental lives of animals. He wrote about non-humans, especially monkeys, apes, cats and dogs, as experiencing pleasure, pain, terror, suspicion, fear, jealousy, self-complacency, pride, curiosity, anxiety, grief, dejection, despair, joy, love, devotion, sulkiness, anger, disdain, disgust, patience, surprise and astonishment. If he were right about even a part of this catalogue, he showed his contemporaries that animals are much more like them than they cared to admit.

The sort of understanding Darwin had becomes a reality to us when we know and love a pet. The student of animal behaviour Konrad Lorenz said that nobody could assess the mental qualities of a dog without having once possessed the love of one. And he added that the same applies to many other animals, such as jack-daws, parrots, geese and monkeys.

Maurice Burton (1978) wrote a book full of anecdotes of the behaviour of animals which suggested to him, by analogy with ourselves, that animals, particularly mammals and birds, experi-ence or show gratitude, compassion, friendliness, faithfulness, anticipation, grief, helpfulness and even heroism. The more we become acquainted with animals the more we tend to attribute to them experiences analogous to our own. We may then ask our-selves questions such as 'What must it be like to be a hen living in a battery cage?' We cannot, of course, have the experience of the hen. We can only imagine its possible experience.

But we have to be careful in using analogies of this sort. Who, one might ask, would like to be a blind mole living all one's life underground? It is not a very appealing lifestyle to us. But we have no reason to suppose such an existence for the mole is a miserable one. On the other hand we have good reasons to be concerned for sheep crowded on ships in small pens on a sea voyage from Australia to the Middle East to make money at the Australian end and to satisfy particular religious rites of killing animals for con-sumption at the end of the journey. Maybe there are lots of unnat-ural things we do to sheep, but this must be one of the most unnatural and one that causes great suffering.

Darwin gave two reasons for supposing that animals have feel-ings akin to ours. One was their biological similarity; the similar aspects of the nervous system and other bodily organ-systems. We are like them because we evolved from the same forebears and inherited their sorts of organs. So it is reasonable to suppose that the brain which is the centre of our feelings is also a centre of feel-ing for them. Secondly he attributed feelings to animals for the same reasons that we attribute feelings to our fellow humans. When a human cries in pain I recognise in that cry what I also associate with pain in my experience.

As we shall see later, Darwin was on the right track in his arguments about the feelings of animals. His first reason above for attributing feelings to animals was given strong emphasis during the Enlightenment by Voltaire who wrote:

> There are barbarians who seize this dog, who so greatly surpasses man in fidelity and friendship, and nail him down to a table and dissect him alive, to show you the mesaraic veins! You discover in him *all the same organs of feeling as in yourself.* Answer me, mechanist, has nature arranged all the springs of feeling in this animal *to the end that he might not feel?* (Singer 1976, p. 220)

There is a difference between us and non-human animals concerning their feelings. They cannot tell us in words when they are in pain. This is also true of humans such as infants who cannot speak. Yet we do not doubt they suffer pain when hurt.

The moral implication is that in so far as a human and a member of another species are similar, they should be treated similarly. If the suffering of a whale when harpooned with a grenade is much the same as the suffering of a human being wounded with a grenade, then we should attach a similar concern to both sufferings. This we return to later.

The changing view about sentience in animals

In hunter-gatherer societies people do not make a sharp distinction between the human and the non-human. No strict hierarchy exists between humans and non-human animals. Many such societies believed that their ancestors had been members of other species. The notion of the Dreamtime in Australian Aborigines emphasises the oneness of all things. Interconnectedness and relatedness are more crucial than distinctness. A similar concept pervades the worldview of American Indians.

Buddhism stresses the unity and continuity of all life, which is an essential element of belief in reincarnation. All that suffer share the same fate. Animals are fellow-beings to humankind hence the vegetarianism of Buddhists. Plato believed in the transmigration of souls from humans to animals and vice versa, as did also Pythagoras. Democritus and Lucretius, on the other hand, with their materialistic theory of nature, deprived living organisms of sentience. Aristotle's concept of the Great Chain of Being in the living world with humans on the top is ambiguous, with both continuity and hierarchy emphasised. Yet Aristotle endowed both human and non-human animals with *anima sensitiva,* the soul of sensation. He thus recognised their capacity for experiencing pleasure and pain. But only humans possessed *anima rationalis* or rationality. Humans are rational animals. Animals are not. This belief led Greek philosophers, particularly the Stoics, to argue that humans may do anything they like to animals. Yet the issue of rationality has no moral relevance whatsoever (Sorabji 1993).

For Judaism, the biblical story of creation stresses the intrinsic value of every living creature (God saw that it was good) but gave a special status to humans in the doctrine of *imago Dei* in Genesis 1:26. Humans and humans alone are made in the image of God. As Cobb (1991a) points out, the Christian habit of accentuating only this reflects more an arrogance than a balanced reading of the story. Humans have a particular significance, but that is placed within the context that became largely lost in the course of Christian thought. The context focuses on the goodness or intrinsic value of all life.

Jesus depicted God as loving sparrows and caring for them as well as humans. They too are subjects and not just objects devoid of sentience. Moreover, he said that a human being is worth more than many sparrows, implying that a sparrow's worth is more than zero.

Other stories in the Christian tradition may seem to give a different picture, such for example as the story of the demons cast out of the demoniac by Jesus. The story tells that they then entered a herd of swine which hurled themselves into the lake at the bottom of a hill to drown. Peter Singer (1976) comments on this story: 'Jesus himself showed indifference to the fate of non-humans when he induced 2000 swine to hurl themselves into the sea' (p. 209). But did this event happen as it is recorded? In Victorian times the narrative of the Gadarene swine became a battleground between biologist professor Thomas Huxley and prime minister William Gladstone. Huxley contended that the narrative was fiction. Gladstone affirmed it as literal fact. However, there is probably no New Testament scholar of any standing today who would maintain that the demoniac was actually possessed of a legion of demons and that they were transferred to a herd of swine. Jesus can be relieved of any responsibility for the fate of the swine. He had no control over them, though he did seem to exercise control over the man. Many Christians devalue non-human animals because of the doctrine of *imago Dei,* that man was made in the image of God. This devaluation cannot be attributed to Jesus. His valuation of nature suggests he would have had compassion for pigs and battery hens as well as humans.

The Stoic view that humans had no responsibility to animals was introduced into Christian thought by St Augustine. In late Medieval Europe much thinking about nature was influenced by St Thomas Aquinas, himself deeply influenced by Aristotle. But his thought became dominant only later. St Thomas is quite explicit that it is all right for humans to kill animals for food and to use them for any useful human purpose. Yet he acknowledges that 'irrational animals are sensible to pain'. And he instructs that we should not be cruel to animals. The reason he gives is that this could lead to cruelty toward human beings. This view did not prevent Pope Pius IX in the middle of the nineteenth century from refusing to sanction a society for the Prevention of Cruelty to Animals to be established in Rome, on the grounds that to do so would imply that humans have duties toward animals (Passmore 1975, p. 203).

As contrasted with the official theology of the church in popular medieval tradition, many legends associate saintliness with kindness to animals. Jerome has his friendly lion, as does Androcles. The most famous example of friendship with animals is St Francis who regarded all creatures as his friends to be loved and cared for in their own right. He spoke of the birds as his sisters and is said to have fed wolves.

The scholasticism of the Aristotelian-Thomistic view was not the only worldview in medieval Europe. There were two other contenders for a worldview at that time: a materialistic or mechanistic philosophy derived from Democritus and Lucretius on the one hand; and an organic view of nature which went under various names such as the hermetic, the alchemical and magic view of nature. In the sixteenth and seventeenth centuries modern science came into being partly as the outcome of a three-cornered struggle between these views. Variants of the organic view were put forward by people such as Ficino, Bruno, Telesio, Campanella, Della Porta, Paracelsus and Fludd. For them nature was a living whole. In some of their philosophies all nature was taken to be sentient. Contrary to the scholastic view, humanity was placed within an enchanted nature rather than above a soulless nature. The organic view promoted scientific experimentation and a compassionate view of the creation. The Aristotelian-Thomistic view did not do so. There may have been many reasons. The gap the latter saw between humans and non-humans did not lead to a compassionate view of nature. And the teaching by authority and deductive logic is the antithesis of science with its emphasis on observation and inductive logic.

The ultimate winners in this three-cornered contest were the mechanistic thinkers. Their views were, in due course, made quite explicit by Descartes and were embraced by the church. The organic view was vigorously condemned by the dominant cultural force at the time, which was the church. From then onwards the mechanistic view of nature and the rule of humans over nature go hand in hand.

During the Enlightenment, Voltaire and Rousseau espoused a more compassionate attitude to non-human animals. On the other hand Immanuel Kant in 1780 declared in his lectures that animals are not self-conscious, and are there as means to human ends. In that same year Jeremy Bentham gave what Singer (1976, p. 222) calls the definitive answer to Kant: 'The question is not, Can they *reason*? nor Can they *talk*? but Can they *suffer*?' Writing in 1789 Jeremy Bentham declared: 'The day may come when the rest of the animal creation may acquire those rights which never

FEELINGS OF ANIMALS 45

could have been withheld from them but by the hand of tyranny'
(Nash 1990, p. 23). Bentham added that the time will come when
humanity will extend its mantle over every thing which breathes.
We are still waiting.

The history of human attitudes to animals is, as Passmore
(1975, p. 217) says, discouraging, in so far as it took two thousand years for humans in the West to agree that it is wrong to be
cruel to animals. Yet it is encouraging that human attitudes did
eventually change with some rapidity, so we now have societies
for the prevention of cruelty to animals in many lands.

Why attribute feelings to animals?

It is not enough to argue that because animals behave like us in
some respects, therefore they must have feelings akin to ours.
The trouble about that alone as an argument is that robots can
be made that simulate many of the activities of animals. A robot
that has 'arms' and 'sensors' that can accurately put rivets and bolts
into an automobile and screw nuts into position is performing an
intelligent action. It is mimicking a human being whose similar
action we would describe as intelligent. But that behaviour is not
a reason for attributing feelings to the robot. Stuart Sutherland
(1985) considers that, so far as we know, there is no behaviour, no
matter how complex, that could not be exhibited by a computer
without consciousness.

As was indicated earlier, Darwin did not make the mistake of
attributing feelings to animals simply on the basis that they behave
like us. In our own time Searle (1992) makes the same point when
he says:

> I am completely convinced that my dog, as well as other higher
> animals, has conscious mental states, such as visual experiences,
> feelings of pain, and sensations of thirst and hunger, and cold and
> heat. Now why am I so convinced of that? The standard answer is
> because of the dog's behaviour, because by observing his behaviour
> I infer that he has mental states like my own. I think this answer is
> mistaken. It isn't just because the dog behaves in a way that is
> appropriate to having conscious mental states, but also because I
> can see that the causal basis of the behaviour in the dog's physiol-

ogy is relevantly like my own...it is in the combination of these two facts that I can see that the behaviour is appropriate and that it has the appropriate *causation* in the underlying physiology. (p. 73)

My attribution of consciousness to other human beings involves similar reasoning. They behave as I do in many situations and I know that they have a physiology that is similar to mine. Since I have feelings in these situations I attribute feelings to them also. When people tell me that they have the terrible pain of kidney colic, I know something as to what that must feel like because I have experienced kidney colic. I don't have their pain but I empathise with it because I know what it is to have such a pain. I can be less sure about the feeling of kidney colic in my cat, though I am pretty sure it is in great pain when I know that is its problem. Empathy, even with members of our own species, has its limits. Some women argue that men have no inkling of the experiences of childbirth and menstruation. If there are gender barriers within our species in sharing feelings, it is even more likely that there will be some barriers between ourselves and other species.

The more we know about the physiology and biochemistry of animals, the more similar they seem to be to one another. The anti-anxiety agents benzodiazepines have an effect on non-human animals similar to that which they have on humans. Sensory receptors for these chemicals have been found in all vertebrates except cartilaginous fishes such as sharks. This suggests that a wide range of vertebrates may experience some sort of suffering akin to anxiety in humans. A wide range of vertebrates also are known to have 'reward circuits' in their brains. These are pathways of nerves involved in feelings of pleasure following a reward. We need not cease our concerns below the vertebrates. Nervous systems and sense organs exist in all animals from jellyfish and above, and even single-celled animals are sentient. We might not be far wrong if we postulate a gradation in sensitivity depending upon the complexity of the sensory system.

On the basis of similarities in physiology between humans and non-humans, the American Veterinary Medical Association recognised the following sorts of suffering in animals (Donnelley & Nolan 1990, p. 14):

Pain: an unpleasant sensory and emotional experience associated with damage of tissues.

Distress: a state in which an animal is unable to adapt to an altered environment (e.g., abnormal food) or to altered internal states (e.g., stomach lesions or high blood pressure).

Discomfort: a state in which the animal *seems* unadapted to a new environment. These might be physical or social changes and are indicated by changes in physiology and behaviour.

Anxiety: a state of increased arousal and alertness prompted by an unknown danger, such as a cat might experience on a visit to the veterinarian.

Fear: a response to a known danger present in the immediate environment.

An animal may experience a number of these states at the same time. For example, an animal in pain is often distressed and may also be fearful when the pain is associated with a certain stimulus such as the arrival of a certain experimenter. Fear can exacerbate pain. Taking a pet to the veterinarian may produce this mixed response.

It would be nice if we were able to measure the suffering of an animal by some physiological or biochemical index. As yet there is no simple way of doing this (Dawkins 1980). Some suffering in animals appears to be caused by stress. Stress has its biochemical indicators. An animal that is confronted by a predator or is confined in a small cage exhibits the first indication of stress, which is the alarm phase. It seeks to fight or flee. A particular part of the nervous system, the sympathetic nervous system, is activated, causing the adrenal glands to secrete two hormones, adrenalin (= epinephrine) and noradrenalin (= norepinephrine), which give rise to the flight or fight syndrome. Heart rate increases as does the rate of breathing. For an animal in the wild, like a zebra being stalked by a lion, this is the stage when the animal flees or fights.

However, if the stress continues, as it would for an animal confined in a small cage, a new set of hormones is secreted from the pituitary gland, notably adreno-cortico-trophic-hormone (ACTH). Its presence in the blood is an indicator of the second phase of stress, known as the resistance stage. ACTH stimulates the adrenal glands to produce a number of hormones such as cortisone and hydrocortisone. These help to keep the body provided with a source of energy in the form of sugar. Eventually the animal enters the final stage of stress, which is exhaustion. The activity of various glands such as the thyroid begin to decline and in young animals growth slows down, resistance to disease is lowered, digestion is impaired and stomach ulcers may develop. None of these symptoms seems to develop in the zebra in the wild, as its stress is short-lived. Hence the intriguing title of Sapolsky's (1994) book: *Why Zebras Don't Get Ulcers*.

By measuring symptoms of stress the physiologist may reasonably infer that she is measuring symptoms associated with suffering or that precede suffering. These symptoms typically occur when animals are crowded in cages or are transported in various sorts of ways. We may then infer from their symptoms that these animals are suffering.

Hormone levels have been studied in sheep subjected to various farm routines such as being put in a truck or chased by a dog. There was a rise in the level of cortisone-type hormones. But none of these routines had nearly as much effect as separating the sheep from the rest of the flock. Shearing a sheep, when it is taken away from the flock, led to higher hormone levels even than slaughtering it, when it is together with other animals. When a cockerel is confronted with a strange cockerel or when handled by a human being, its heart rate increases. The so-called sport of cock fights is cruel, even before the fight begins. When sheep, cattle and pigs are moved to a new environment, or given a different diet, the electrical activity of the forebrain shows characteristic changed patterns indicating stress (Dawkins 1980, pp. 60-8). One wonders what sheep suffer when they are transported overseas.

Sometimes the behaviour of an animal indicates that it is probably suffering some distress or pain. Polar bears, foxes and tigers, for example, often pace backwards and forwards in their cages in zoos. They tend to use a fixed pathway which becomes worn away where the animal has persistently gone round in a circle or figure of eight.

Psychologists and ethologists who study animal behaviour have, for the most part, been unwilling to attribute consciousness to non-human animals. There are many reasons for their reluctance, a major one being that it is impossible to prove conclusively whether or not an animal is conscious. We know that lots of activities go on in our own brains of which we are not conscious. Is it not possible that all mental activity in animals is unconscious? Donald Griffin has written extensively on the minds of animals and on what he considers to be reasons for attributing consciousness to them, not just to apes and porpoises but even to honey bees and other invertebrates (Griffin 1981, 1984, 1992). Griffin is an ethologist who has become convinced, in his detailed study of animal behaviour, that animals exhibit consciousness. They think, remember, anticipate and intend. Particularly impressive for him is the extent to which animals are able to adapt complex behaviour to varying and often unpredictable circumstances.

A green-backed heron breaks a twig into small pieces and uses it as bait for fishing. It casts the twig into the water and watches it intently until an unfortunate minnow investigates. The behaviour of the heron is immensely flexible. She may drop the bait from an overhanging perch or from the water's edge, retrieving it if it floats away. When the minnow investigates the twig the heron dives on it.

A hungry chimpanzee walking through his native rain forest in the Ivory Coast comes upon a large nut of *Panda oleosa* lying on the ground under a panda tree. These nuts are far too hard to open with his hands or teeth. They can only be cracked open by pounding them with a hard piece of rock. Very few such rocks are available in the forest. However, he walks for about 80 metres straight to another tree where several days ago he had cracked open a panda nut with a chunk of granite. He carries this rock back to the nut he has found, places the nut in a crotch between two buttress roots, and cracks it open with a few well-aimed blows.

Concerning both the heron and the chimpanzee Griffin (1992) asks: 'Must we reject, or repress, any suggestions that the chimpanzee or the heron thinks consciously about the tasty food it manages to obtain by these coordinated actions?' (p. 2). He sees no reason why we should reject such a proposition any more than we would reject such a proposition about the behaviour of a human being performing similar tasks. The point here is not that intelligent behaviour implies being conscious. But there is nothing to rule out that possibility. It is necessary to make the distinction between intelligent behaviour and consciousness. There are many complex tasks that humans do without being conscious. So we need more than complexity of behaviour before we conclude a particular set of activities are conscious.

Beavers are notable for their adaptive behaviour when circumstances change. For example, two beavers were kept in an enclosure where the water level was regulated by an outlet pipe with perforated holes through which water escaped. After two weeks the beavers began to plug the holes with peeled twigs which had been gnawed off obliquely at both ends by the beavers, and planed down in such a way that they exactly fitted the holes. When the sticks were removed the beavers made new ones and again blocked up the holes, thus raising the water level again (Griffin 1992, p. 88).

These examples of behaviour adapted to meet changing circumstances indicate that the behaviour is not rigidly determined. This adaptability suggests, though it does not prove, conscious thinking. Adaptability of behaviour to changing circumstances is not just an attribute of birds and mammals but is characteristic of the behaviour of wasps and many other arthropods (Griffin 1984, p. 111).

Intentional planning and the communication of simple thoughts seems to guide the behaviour of the African greater honey-guide. These birds are fond of the wax from honeycombs and they can digest beeswax. However, they cannot open bee nests. In an apparent effort to obtain beeswax they cooperate with human beings and perhaps other animals that tear open the bee nests to take honey and still leave plenty of honeycomb for the honey-guides. There is no doubt that in many parts of Africa honey-guides lead humans who are searching for bee nests to where the nests are. When the bird is ready to be a guide, it may search out a person and starts to make a series of calls, waiting for the person to approach nearer. As the person approaches it flies off to another tree, waits there, calling until the person gets closer, then repeats the process again and again. When the nest is reached the bird perches on a nearby tree until the person has departed with his loot of honeycomb. It then comes down from the tree and begins to feed on what is left. The distance it travels may be several kilometres. Many studies of this behaviour indicate that the bird keeps a memory of a bee nest it has found and leads the person on a direct route.

Behaviourists try to translate such behaviour in terms of a sequence of stimulus and response without any consciousness being involved. Griffin (1992, p. 169) argues that the resulting account becomes more and more unwieldy as more is learned about the details of the behaviour of the bird. To assume a simple conscious intent to lead the follower to the bees' nest and get food after it has opened the nest, is a more parsimonious and reasonable interpretation.

It is now known that animals communicate with their own species in quite complex and versatile ways. The most outstanding example amongst invertebrates is communication among honey bees. Ever since the pioneering studies on honey bees by von Frisch in the 1920s, many investigators have accumulated evidence about the extraordinary ways bees communicate to one another in the hive. By means of complex dances on the vertical surface of the honeycomb they are able to communicate the horizontal distance, direction and the concentration of the source of food they have discovered. Some sort of 'internal map' seems to exist in the brain. Bees can also communicate to each other the location and suitability of potential localities for a new hive when swarming. Again they do this by complex dances. Individual bees are swayed by the information they receive to the extent that, after inspection of individual locations, worker bees change their preference and dance for the superior place rather than one they first discovered or was communicated to them by their mates. Eventually the bees reach a consensus after which the swarm as a whole flies off to the chosen place. The bees do not appear to be acting as programmed robots. Theirs is not a totally stereotyped behaviour. If the 'language' were in words rather than in dances and were the bees closer to the size of a dog, we would be strongly inclined to attribute to them similar experiences to those humans have when they communicate whether to go to this place or that (Griffin 1992, pp. 178-94).

Griffin considers that one of the clearest examples of communication in animals that suggests conscious thinking is the alarm call of the vervet monkey. These monkeys live in groups in forests and open areas in Africa. When they see dangerous predators they make three different alarm calls in response to three sorts of predator: leopards, eagles and snakes. Alarm calls for leopards cause vervets to run into trees, where they seemed safe from attack. Alarm calls for eagles causes them to look up into the air or run into bushes. Alarm calls for snakes caused them to stand on their hind legs and look into the grass. There is a best way to escape from each of these predators and the alarm calls elicit the appropriate response. A generalised response call would be ineffective as there would be no point, for example, in climbing a tree if the danger is from a python.

By recording and later playing back alarm calls to vervets in the wild, it has been possible to elicit their responses in the absence of any predator, indicating that it is the call, not the sight of the predator, that elicits the response. One call might mean climb a tree, another—look into the grass. Alarm calls function as semantic signals. Semantics is the word used in linguistics to mean the attribution of meaning to symbols. The three different calls are symbols that have three different meanings to vervet monkeys (Cheney & Seyfarth 1990; Seyfarth & Cheney 1992).

Extensive studies of vervet monkeys by Cheney and Seyfarth led them to the conclusion that the vervets' view of the world is very different from ours. Though they make use of abstract concepts and have motives and desires, their mental states do not seem to be accessible to themselves in the sense in which we regard ourselves as being self-aware. Nor are they able to attribute mental states to others or to recognise that others' behaviour is also caused by motives, beliefs and desires. Be that as it may, can we confidently conclude that communication in vervet monkeys is conscious? One thing would seem to be clear and that is that the origin of their complex behaviour conforms to mechanistic programming by natural selection. Those vervets survive best that have the best means of communication. But as in other examples, previously given, compexity of behaviour in itself does not demonstrate the probability of conscious states. However, it can be supportive when combined with other evidence, as is indicated later.

According to Griffin (1992, p. 232) experiments on the way apes can be trained to communicate with each other and with humans by means of symbols demonstrate an evolutionary continuity between human and non-human communication and thinking. Apes have been taught to use over 100 signs developed for communication by deaf people. A sign was used by trainers in the presence of the object for which the sign stands. Other investigators trained apes to use plastic tokens which the apes would use to obtain certain objects, such as a banana. Other investigators trained apes to use a keyboard connected to a computer. The ape learns which key it must touch to get a certain object. Each key has on it a particular pattern as a symbol. The symbols are semantic representations. But can apes use syntax, that is, can they string symbols or words together to make some sort of sentence? This ability seems to be beyond apes with one possible exception. There is some evidence that one pigmy chimpanzee could use a combination of a few symbols together to communicate with another chimpanzee and with humans (Griffin 1992, pp. 218-32).

At some stage in the evolution of our genus *Homo*, the capacity for speech evolved, that is to say, communication by means of a language of words. Among animals on Earth today there seems to be a gap between the one creature who can speak and all other animals. The capacity for speech is genetically determined and is located in two areas of the brain. The front area is called Broca's area. It controls the 'motor' performance involved in speech, that is to say the formation of words into sentences that are then given voice by the larynx. The rear one is called Wernicke's area. It is involved in the comprehension of language. A person who has a stroke in Wernicke's area cannot understand words or form sentences whereas a person with a stroke in Broca's area can understand speech but cannot speak.

How far back in our evolutionary history can we find evidence of the existence of these speech areas in the brain? There is one source of evidence from the past. The blood vessels of these areas in touch with the inner surface of the cranial cavity make their imprint on the surface of the cranial cavity. Anthropologist Philip Tobias considers that these imprints are sufficiently evident in the skull of *Homo habilis* to suggest that the speech areas were developed in this our ancient ancestor of a million years ago (Denton 1993, p. 134). There is no evidence for the existence of such areas in the brain of chimpanzees. It is not that they lack vocal apparatus for speech. It is just that their brains are unable to produce and use grammar.

The ability to communicate by speech gave to us the capacity for cultural evolution that makes the difference between cave people of half a million years ago and modern humans. Cultural evolution is the transfer of information through non-genetic means, such as by imitation, and learned behaviour and for ourselves it is information that is communicated by speech.

So far I have given four reasons which, if taken together, suggest that animals have consciousness:

1   Their behaviour is similar to ours, which we know is conscious for us.
2   Their physiology and biochemistry are similar to ours.
3   Adaptable behaviour is explained more simply and directly by assuming that it is conscious.
4   Complex means of communication between animals suggest consciousness.
5   There is a fifth reason, which has to do with evolution. This argument is put succinctly by Helena Cronin (1992):

> I am convinced that, say, chimpanzees are conscious. Why? Well, I know I am conscious, I know a mere 500,000 generations separate me from my chimpanzee cousin, and I know evolutionary innovations don't just spring into existence full-blown, certainly not innovations as truly momentous as our haunting elusive private world. (p. 14)

Her argument is that just as all human organs have a long evolutionary history, consciousness must surely have a long evolutionary history.

6 Marian Stamp Dawkins (1993, p. 147) adds a sixth reason which suggests that animals are conscious.

It is the demonstration that animals have a point of view in which what happens to them *matters* to them. She argues that the most crucial aspect of feeling and emotion for us is that it *matters* to us. If we are in pain it matters to us that it should go away. Is there evidence that animals too care about what happens to them? Dawkins says there is. An animal that will do anything to escape from a small cage or to cross an electrified grid to get a female is showing what matters to it, just as much as humans who give their last mite to save the destruction of their beloved school. A telling example she gives is an experiment with mice and hamsters. Each animal was put in a glass container. A steady stream of tobacco smoke was blown into the containers down a glass tube. The animals soon learned to stop the stream of smoke from coming into their containers by bunging up the ends of the glass tubes with their faeces. Several of them actually asphyxiated themselves because the smoky stream of air was also their only supply of oxygen. It seemed that they regarded what was being done to them as something to be avoided by any means available.

We tend to view living things quite differently from dead things or material objects such as rocks and chairs. What makes the difference? Hartshorne (1934, p. 13) suggests that we regard the dead or material things as interesting only to ourselves, whereas when we look upon the things as alive we feel at least a germ of empathy with them. We imagine ourselves feelingly in their place. We wonder at their possible pleasures, pains, desires and interests. Besides being interesting to us or others, the living creature presents itself as interesting to itself. This is the vivid and unmistakable experience I have when a speck, such as a tiny mite on the page I am reading, convinces me that it is no mere speck, but a living sentient creature.

What is it like to be my cat?

I wish I really knew. I would then be in a better position to make his life happier. But I know quite a lot. I get this information in a similar way to how I get information about the feelings of humans I know. I know when my cat feels hungry and wants his dinner. I know when he is in pain and needs to visit the veterinarian. I only wish I were able to explain to him that the visit will be good for him. I cannot communicate that information but I can communicate to him my concern and comfort. I think he is lonely at times when I am away for many hours. I find him waiting at the front door when I return. Loneliness seems to be converted to joy as he rolls over in greeting me and purrs at high volume. Maybe he also experiences a feeling of gratefulness to me on such occasions, but I am less sure of that. Although he enjoys lying in the sun on a cool day, he will often leave his comfortable lair to be in my company at the opposite end of the house. I suspect that at a certain point he enjoys my company and attention more than the sun's warmth. If he can get both together he seems to like that combination.

Of course I cannot really know what it is like to be my cat in the sense that I know what it is like to be me. But I know no argument to make me think that my knowledge of my cat's feelings is, in any major way, different from that of a fellow human's feelings. There are bigger gaps, to be sure. He sees in black and white. I have some idea of what that is like when I watch a black and white movie. He also has quite a different range of smell to mine. In so far as he has ideas about me, perhaps it is that I am just a big cat. I am certainly not the dog next door nor the magpie on the balcony. They are in a different category. I suspect that my cat does not reflect on what it is like to be a cat or the dog next door. At least we have no evidence that a cat has this sort of 'self-consciousness'.

Avid cat owners claim to know a lot about the feelings of their pets. This sort of understanding strikes a chord of empathy between cat lovers. How else does one account for the phenomenal sales of best sellers such as *The Cat Who Came For Christmas* by Cleveland Amory?

If my cat could talk I would know immeasurably more about his feelings. But that alas is denied me. Dennett (1991) quotes Wittgenstein as saying: 'if a lion could talk, we could not understand him' (p. 447). On the contrary, argues Dennett, we could understand him just fine. But it wouldn't tell us much about ordinary lions that cannot talk. The mind of a lion that can talk must be very different from one that cannot talk.

Thomas Nagel (1974) wrote about a thought experiment on feelings or consciousness in his widely quoted paper 'What is it Like to Be a Bat?' There is a sufficient gulf between Nagel and a bat for him to conclude that he did not know what it is like to be a bat. But I don't think he would have come to a similar conclusion about his pet cat or dog, if he has one. He was really saying that the subjective experience of a bat is the bat's alone and not his. But is not the position of the bat in relation to himself analogous to the relation of a human friend to himself? Nagel's view has been challenged, as for example by Dennett (1991, pp. 441-5) who argues that there is a lot that we can know about what it is like to be a bat. For example, by trying hard enough we can find out about the bat's perceptual world, such as that bats are not bothered by the loud squeaks they emit to produce echoes for echolocation of objects and prey because they shut down their ears in perfect timing with the squeaks. I feel pretty sure that the curator of bats in the zoo who nurses injured bats that are sent to her by concerned citizens would know a lot about the feelings of a bat.

We are denied the bat's experience of echolocation, the dog's sense of smell that enables it to distinguish between clothing worn by different people, the capacity of honey bees and some other insects to discriminate the plane of polarization of light and the capacity of sharks to be so sensitive to electric currents that they can detect prey by the electrical potentials from their heartbeats. Many animals have sensory abilities that are different from our own. But they have other sensory abilities in common with us, such as some taste and smell. We can apply the same principles to the bat as we apply to ourselves as we relate to other humans.

It would be nice for our understanding if conscious experience were tied to some particular electrical activity in some particular part of the brain. But there is little evidence for this, at least as yet. If there were we could then see if non-human animals showed similar brain activity to humans for certain behaviours.

Experiences animals have

Animals are like us in that they seem to experience pleasure and pain, terror and fear, suspicion, jealousy, self-complacency and pride. They sulk, they love their children. They seem curious and adventurous. They seem to want to communicate. They get lonely. They grieve. The latter seems to be the case with chimpanzees that Jane Goodall (1971, 1986) studied in Gombe Reserve. When his mother, Flo, died, the young chimpanzee Flint exhibited many of the patterns of behaviour we associate with grief in humans. He avoided others, stopped eating, and spent many hours each day sitting in a hunched posture rocking back and forth. Eventually he died. Although chimpanzees grieve at the loss of close friends, they do not seem to recognize the same mental states of grief in others. As a result they are unable to share their grief or show empathy toward grieving mates.

The songs of birds give aesthetic pleasure to humans. But do birdsongs give aesthetic pleasure to birds? Hartshorne (1973) made many recordings of the songs of birds around the world and became convinced that they are so structured as to avoid monotony. A bird that has few notes spaces them at longer intervals than a bird that has many notes. According to Joan Hall-Craggs (in Hinde 1969) the musical construction is identical to that which we find in our own music. Why deny the bird the pleasure of enjoying birdsong?

Self-consciousness

A distinction is sometimes made between perception or awareness of anything, such as the presence of food, and reflection on such awareness. These have been called perceptual consciousness and reflective consciousness (Griffin 1992, p. 10). Some people, for example Popper and Eccles (1977), claim that reflective consciousness is a unique human capability or perhaps one that is shared with the great apes. Reflective consciousness is what some people call self-awareness — not only to know but to know that one knows. Reflective consciousness involves a form of introspection, that is, thinking about one's own feelings and thoughts. A human infant is aware of lots of things, such as hunger, pain and touch. But it probably does not do much if any reflection on these perceptions. That comes later in life. All mature humans presumably reflect on what they are aware of to some extent, but the degree of reflection seems to vary enormously. A hermit in his cave presumably does an enormous amount of reflection compared to a drinker in the corner pub. May there not also be a gradation in reflective awareness as we go from dogs to monkeys to apes to pre-humans such as *Australopithecus* to ourselves? There is no sound biological reason as yet to draw sharp lines anywhere. In human history different levels of self-reflection seem to have been achieved at different stages of cultural evolution.

A being who is self-aware will know that he or she will die. Presumably such a being arose from ancestors who did not know this or hardly knew it. So evidence of death-awareness is evidence of self-awareness. The earliest evidence we have of death-awareness in humans is in the Neanderthal sub-species of *Homo sapiens*. The most ancient burial is in Palestine of about 100 000 years ago. Several bodies were laid in graves cut in the floor of a cave and were accompanied by offerings of food and weapons. The graves of other Neanderthals in Europe also suggest ceremonial burial of the dead (Dobzhansky 1967, p. 69). *Homo sapiens* evolved about half a million years ago and perhaps death-awareness existed much earlier than 100 000 years ago, but we just do not have the necessary evidence from graves earlier than 100 000 years ago.

Is it possible to argue for the existence of some form of death-awareness in non-human animals? There are many accounts of seeming grief of pair-bonded animals following the death of one of them. Denton (1993) refers to accidental violent death in a chimpanzee troupe in the Gombe stream. The whole troupe witnessed how one of their number Rix fell and broke his neck on a boulder. The males began a complex series of displays, standing erect, stamping the ground and tearing at bushes and trees and throwing stones. Each chimpanzee stopped and stared at the corpse, calling to and embracing each other. Some twelve individuals gathered around the body in the form of a circle. The apparent distress of the chimpanzees lasted for more than three hours, after which the top-ranking chimpanzee led the troupe away (p. 144). Were the chimpanzees grasping at the difference between life and death?

Concern over the dead and ceremonial burial of the dead exemplify a pre-rational source of the meaning of the self. Pre-rational sources of meaning became replaced by rational ones with a conflict between the two ever present. Perhaps we can speak of full self-consciousness appearing for the first time only by the first millennium BC, when quite independently in China, India, Persia, Greece and Israel spiritual leaders arose who proposed new ways of ordering the *whole* of their experience. From then on we find people devoting a great deal of their time to reflecting upon the meaning of life and death.

If an animal reflects it would be difficult for us to know what its thoughts are because it has no language to tell us. However, some chimpanzees can recognise themselves in a mirror. After becoming familiar with mirrors, chimpanzees were anaesthetised and while they were unconscious a mark was placed on a part of the head that they could not see directly. On awakening they paid no attention to the mark until a mirror was provided. They then touched the mark and gave every indication of recognising that the mark was on their own bodies. Seeing a mark, they reflected that it had something to do with themselves. Although orangutans responded to mirrors in this way, efforts to elicit such responses from monkeys, gibbons and gorillas have failed (Griffin 1992, p. 249). We would seem to need to discover other ways of penetrating the mind of animals to know to what extent they may reflect on their perceptions.

The age at which a human child recognises itself in a mirror is controversial. It may not be until it is one year old. It is a year or more after that when a human child refers to itself with the use of pronouns. Presumably it is then self-conscious.

So we may think of reflective consciousness or self-awareness as a developing capacity from the new-born child to adult, and from early humans of half a million years ago to ourselves. Within these limits there is surely a continuity which may extend below to pre-human creatures.

The right to live

Billions of animals are killed every year for food for humans. Most of these animals are chickens and mammals. The physiologists Francois Magendie and his student Claude Bernard institutionalised the practice of using animals in research in the first half of the nineteenth century. Since then research using animals has grown. Today over 100 million animals are used in research laboratories all over the world. Some 85 per cent are rats and mice. Frogs, hamsters, guineapigs, rabbits, pigeons, chickens, dogs, cats, pigs and primates constitute most of the rest. These animals are used in a variety of ways: in physiological and medical research; in the production and standardisation of biological products such as vaccines, insulin and antitoxins; in the diagnosis of disease; in school and university education; in testing toxicity of new chemicals and a variety of new products from pesticides and cleansers to cosmetics. One estimate indicates that about half of all animals used in experiments experience an appreciable discomfort. They have the right not to be made to suffer unnecessarily.

In the last 20 years there has been much criticism of the use of animals by humans. A number of philosophers have argued the rights and wrongs of this, notably Peter Singer (1976, 1991), Tom Regan (1983) and Bernard Rollin (1989). The debate involves a revaluation of the moral status of animals, the meaning of animal pain and suffering and the benefits of the knowledge gained from experiments using animals. If animals have no feelings or consciousness then this debate is misguided and pointless. The main argument for endowing rights on non-human animals is the same as that for endowing rights on humans. It is that they have conscious feelings. To have feelings is to have intrinsic value. Intrinsic value of an individual is value in itself for itself, quite independent of any value it may have for others (its instrumental value).

There are a number of arguments for animal rights. One group of arguments, such as those of Singer and Regan, are based on the proposition that humans and all animals that warrant moral considerability have equal rights. Singer includes among animals having moral considerability all animals that appear to experience suffering. For him the line is drawn below animals such as crayfish and crabs. Whatever causes suffering in animals is bad. Regan gives equal rights to all mammals but to nothing else, and when he speaks of animals he mostly means mammals. He puts mammals in a different class from all others because of qualities such as entertaining goals and acting deliberately. Both Singer and Regan conclude that the use of animals (usually mammals) for experimental purposes and the use of animals for food, is ethically unacceptable. Instead of using animals for experimental purposes they advocate experiments on tissues in tissue culture. Both are strong advocates of vegetarianism.

A second sort of argument for animal rights does not accept the proposition that all animals (or mammals only in Regan's case) including humans have equal rights. There is a gradation of rights corresponding to a gradation in capacity to feel, and hence a gradation in intrinsic value. So in this view humans have more intrinsic value and therefore more rights than mosquitoes. Chimpanzees and whales have more rights than frogs. This view has been argued by Birch and Cobb (1981), Birch (1993) and Cobb (1991a).

In 1988 a group of theologians, ethicists and scientists were brought together under the auspices of the World Council of Churches to report on an appropriate theology of nature for our time, and an appropriate ethic arising from that theology. The report of this group became known as the Annecy Report, after the name of the town in France where the consultation was held. The report to the WCC became a controversial issue, probably because of its emphasis on the intrinsic value of creatures besides humans and its proposal that, even when respect for animals does not coincide with human benefit, it is still required of Christians. A second reason for the controversy was that the report on ethical attitudes to animals was regarded by some as extremely radical. It has to be borne in mind that Christian churches have emphasised the intrinsic value of humans to the exclusion of other creatures despite the fact that this is a misreading of the Bible. Its tradition has become almost exclusively anthropocentric. The report argued for a less anthropocentric ethic to replace this. It has been published as an appendix in two books (Birch, Eakin & McDaniel 1990; Pinches & McDaniel 1993).

The Annecy Report selected five areas in which there is much suffering of animals and called for changes to reduce this suffering and to enhance the lives of animals. The areas were:

* The manufacture of household and cosmetic products. Items as diverse as cosmetics and detergents and many others are tested on animals in a variety of ways including eye-irritant tests and lethal dose tests.
* The production of items of apparel such as furs and gloves which require the trapping of live animals or their farming. There are alternative items of apparel that do not involve the suffering of animals.
* The production of food. The 'good shepherd' has given way largely to huge business ventures with the goal of raising the largest number of animals in the shortest time. Upward of 4 billion animals are raised for food each year in the US alone. Much of this production involves cruelty to animals.
* The use of animals for entertainment such as circuses, aquatic shows, rodeos, bullfights, cock- and dog-fights and hunting. The animals in these activities are treated as mere ends to human entertainment. The housing, display and transport of these animals involves much cruelty.
* The education of students in schools and universities involves the use of animals such as frogs, mice and rats, which tends to show minimal respect for animals.

The Annecy Report recommended, amongst other concerns, that Christians alter their behaviour such that the suffering of animals is reduced to a minimum by avoiding household products tested on animals, avoiding clothing such as furs that have a history of involving cruelty to animals, avoiding meat and animal products that have been produced on factory farms and in other ways involving cruelty, and avoiding entertainments that treat animals as means to human ends.

The Annecy Report may have asked too much too quickly. At least it pointed to the necessity of a large-scale educational project to get Christians and others to think of their obligation to animals and not to leave such concern simply to secular organisations, many of which do sterling work in this area. It is not a valid argument for Christians to say that animal suffering cannot be a priority when human suffering is still so widespread. If we have to wait for the end of human suffering before we think of other creatures we shall be waiting for ever. It is like someone in the rich world saying we shouldn't help the Third World because we have enough problems of our own at home. Yet it was a Third World scientist, the president of the Indian National Academy of Science, Professor M. Swaminathan, who said: 'If we work for the poor and the penguins simultaneously, we can hope for a better common present and future'.

In some respects the most difficult of all problems we face in our treatment of animals are those in the wild such as kangaroos, elephants, tigers and lions. In every continent the habitats of wild animals are being encroached upon by agriculture. Wild animals are being displaced by domestic cattle, and their habitats are changing mostly to the disadvantage of the wild animals.

Recently a group of people sympathetic to the plight of our nearest relatives amongst the animals, namely the great apes (chimpanzees, gorilla and orangutan) have established the Great Ape Project (Cavalieri & Singer 1993). They hope it will have the clout to argue the case for great apes at the UN, to provide better protection for apes still living. Implementation of the project would spell the end of their use in research, as exhibits in zoos and as objects of entertainment.

The proponents of this project argue for the inclusion of the great apes within the sphere of equal moral consideration with humans. This means, they argue, that the great apes should be treated as equal to humans. Considerations for equality are based on two sets of arguments. The great apes are biologically the closest relatives to humans amongst all animals. Amongst them our closest relative is the chimpanzee. We share 98 per cent of our DNA with the two living species of chimpanzees, the common and the pygmy chimp. The second set of considerations is that the great apes are intelligent beings with a rich and varied social and emotional life. As Jane Goodal writes (in Cavalieri & Singer 1993):

> The postures and gestures with which chimpanzees communicate — such as kissing, embracing, holding hands, patting one another on the back, swaggering, punching, hair pulling, tickling — are not only uncannily like many of our own, but are used in similar contexts and clearly have similar meanings. Two friends may greet with an embrace and a fearful individual may be calmed by a touch, whether they be chimpanzees or humans. Chimpanzees are capable of sophisticated cooperation and complex social manipulation. Like us, they have a dark side to their nature: they can be brutal, they are aggressively territorial, sometimes they engage in a primitive type of warfare. But they also show a variety of helping and care-giving behaviours and are capable of true altruism. (p. 13)

An individual great ape has great intrinsic value. Whether or not its intrinsic value is to be equated with the intrinsic value of humans hardly alters the argument for our responsibility to them. Today fewer than 300 000 chimpanzees survive in the wild. Some 4000 to 5000 live in zoos and laboratories around the world. Chimpanzees in the wild are threatened by millions of humans encroaching on their habitats and by poachers. There is no longer the need, once thought necessary, for keeping large numbers in laboratories, but what to do with those that remain? A chimpanzee can live for 50 years and costs $US 25 000 or more a year to keep, which is more than it costs to keep a prisoner in a jail. There is a housing crisis for chimpanzees. They can't be sent back to Africa, so there is need for chimpanzee sanctuaries, but these are not easy to establish without large sums of money.

The important issue at this stage is that a sufficient number of people become concerned at the plight of our nearest relative, whose intelligence and sensitivities are now well established; that they be given a right to live and fulfil their lives. The Great Ape Project hopes to inspire a sea change in our attitude to the great apes in time to save them. 'We believe that success is possible', says Peter Singer; 'history shows us that there has always been, within

our species, that saving factor: a squad of determined people willing to overcome the selfishness of their own group in order to
advance another's cause' (Vines 1993, p. 42).

The great achievement of the Enlightenment, says Mary
Midgley (1983, p. 51), was to build a theory of the rights of human
beings that made possible enormous advances toward social justice.
A great achievement of our time could be to extend the concepts
of rights and justice to all living creatures, not only in theory but
in the practice of a non-anthropocentric, biocentric ethic.

It may well be that animal liberation will require greater altruism
on our part than any other liberation movement, since animals themselves are incapable of demanding it for themselves or of protesting
against their exploitation by votes, demonstrations or bombs.

The consequences of an animal's having lived, experienced and died

On 1 October 1972, the London *Sunday Times* printed the
obituary of Flo, an adult female chimpanzee who had
lived in the Gombe National Park, Tanzania, and who
had been studied by Jane Goodall for over eleven years. Part of the
obituary read as follows:

> Flo has contributed much to science. She and her large family
> have provided a wealth of information about chimpanzee behav-
> iour, infant development, family relationships, aggression, dom-
> inance, sex... But this should not be the final word. It is true that
> her life was worthwhile because it enriched human understand-
> ing. But even if no one had studied the chimpanzees at Gombe,
> Flo's life, rich and full of vigour and love, would still have had a
> meaning and a significance in the pattern of things.

I believe that. When a much loved pet dies, we experience grief.
Yet we are better off that the beloved animal lived. We also have
a sense that the world is better off. Some of us ask a further question. Is there a sense in which the value of lives that have been
lived are in some way saved, that such value endures? A theist
might put the question this way — did its life make a difference
to God? I explore that thought in Chapter 5.

Conclusion

Throughout history there have been those who thought that non-human animals have no feelings and there have been those who thought they had.

For the most part religions have attributed feelings to non-human animals, but not all have followed the implication of such a belief for an attitude to animals. Scientists, for the most part, have ignored the subjective aspects of feelings. However, much is now being learned about the objective aspects such as physiology and biochemistry of feelings.

There are six main reasons for concluding that non-human animals have feelings: the similarity of their nervous system and biochemistry to ours; their behaviour, which is similar to our behaviour when we experience pleasure or pain; the complex adaptability of animal behaviour; the fact that we who are conscious have an ancestry from non-human animals; the existence of complex systems of communication in many animals, especially in monkeys and apes; and the demonstration that animals have a point of view in which what happens to them matters to them.

A human being does not have the experience of any other human being, yet we empathise with the experience of others. For the same reasons we can empathise with the experience of non-human animals. A pet owner does not have the experiences of his or her pet but nevertheless knows something about the pet's experience by imagination.

Self-consciousness, which is reflective self-awareness, varies greatly in degree between one human being and another. So too there may be degrees of self-consciousness amongst non-human animals. At least there is some evidence that chimpanzees are self-conscious.

The existence of feelings in animals raises the issue of our obligation to animals. In the ethics of intrinsic value the animal is considered to have rights depending upon the richness of its feelings.

3

The Nature of Nature

Emergence of mind from no mind at all is sheer magic.

SEWALL WRIGHT (1964, p. 113)

I remind myself of the old advice that the doctrines which best repay critical examination are those which for the longest period have remained unquestioned.

A. N. WHITEHEAD (1942, p. 207)

Can mind arise from no mind? That question is central to the history of feelings in the evolution of the cosmos. There are just three possible answers to this question. The present dominant view claims that mind is something that emerges in the course of the evolution of life (*emergentism*). From no mind arises mind. A second view is there is no such thing as mind, all is mere matter (*physicalism* or *materialism*). A third view says mind cannot arise from no mind; in some sense mind is part and parcel of all entities in the evolution of the cosmos and the evolution of life; mind and matter are two aspects of the one thing (*panexperientialism*). Both the dualist doctrine of emergence and the doctrine of physicalism dominate the field at present. They are the centre of much controversy, especially since some of their defenders have pointed out seemingly insoluble problems in their own position (see Griffin 1995). The third view (panexperientialism), if not completely ignored by emergentists and physicalists, is dealt with briefly and is usually misunderstood. The implicit, if not explicit, acceptance of the two doctrines of emergence and of physicalism remain unquestioned by many. The time has come to call the unquestioned into question and to consider a third alternative. The question we are really asking is what is the nature of nature? Is it a machine or is it something else? The proposition of this chapter is that it is something else.

The origin of mind

A way of looking at the three alternatives is to ask the question — When did mind arise in cosmic evolution? Physicalism says that it didn't since the only real things are insentient bits of matter. The doctrine of emergence says that mind arose at some point in the evolution of animals, maybe in birds. Before that there was no mind. Panexperientalism asks rhetorically — How could that which is, arise from that which is not? In panexperientialism mind, in some form, and matter have always existed together, all the way back to the Big Bang when the universe is supposed to have begun its history. The proposition is that mind does not arise from no mind — ever.

The question as to the origin of mind is an old one. The

seventeenth-century Hermetic philosopher Tommaso Campanella (1568-1639), himself an ex-Dominican friar, ridiculed the Greek and Roman atomists who declared that sentient creatures arose from non-sentient matter: 'Behold Lucretius the Epicuraean attempting to show, with Democritus, that insentient and inert things can give rise to things with sense and feeling!' (Easlea 1973, p. 254). Campanella was ridiculing the mechanistic orientation of the new science that was being born in his time. A great questioner of the received wisdom of his day, Campanella spent 27 years in prison for attempting to realise a utopian society. On his side against mechanism was his contemporary cosmologist, ex-Dominican friar and heretic Giordano Bruno (1548-1600). Bruno was imprisoned for several years for his heretical views before being burned at the stake on the Campo di Fiori in Rome in 1600. The charge by the Inquisition against him was that he held that God was immanent in the creation, rather than the external creator of a mechanical universe. He was also a Copernican. The Inquisition, by falsely labelling his views as the heresy of pantheism, showed its ignorance of the important distinction between pantheism (which identitifies God and the world) and Bruno's panentheism (which sees God as organically involved with the world but not identified with it).

Bruno was not alone in suffering such a fate for his panentheism. Reymond de Tarrega was murdered in his prison cell in Spain for this heresy in 1371. He was a precursor of Bruno, having similar Hermetic beliefs. The fate of Copernican Bruno must have been a powerful impetus for Galileo to recant his Copernican views a scant 32 years later.

The organic view of Campanella, Bruno and other Hermetic philosophers was incorporated in the Rosicrucian Enlightenment of this period. Its manifesto called for a general reformation in thought, because other reformations had failed. The Protestant Reformation was divided. The Catholic Counter Reformation had taken a wrong turning. The Rosicrucians worked toward a third reformation which they hoped would combine evangelical Christianity with its emphasis on love and the Hermetic tradition with its emphasis on both mind in nature and on scientific exploration (Yates 1972).

By contrast, the exponents of mechanism, particularly Galileo, declared that nature was not alive, that not even tastes, colours and odours really belonged to it. All that was real were the primary qualities of the bits of matter that nature could be reduced to. The real world was matter in motion and nothing more. The machine replaced the organism as a model for understanding the nature of nature. Certainly by the end of the seventeenth century, the belief had established itself that we were living in a world of matter in motion, a completely purposeless world of manipulable matter. It was the denial to nature of all subjectivity, all experience, all feeling. It is what Whitehead (1978, pp. 29, 167) called 'the doctrine of vacuous actuality'.

The eighteenth century is often called the Age of Reason. This name is connected with that century's acceptance of the new scientific, mechanistic worldview. Its greatest thinkers saw their task as eradicating the remaining effects of earlier 'prescientific' and therefore 'irrational' ways of thinking (Cobb 1992). Their removal of the organic view of nature of the Hermetic philosophers and others was by far the most far-reaching effect of the Scientific Revolution. This is the dominant view in philosophy and science today.

The organic as opposed to the mechanistic view of nature

When David Griffin edited *The Reenchantment of Science,* he was making a plea for a return to some of the organic elements of the science that existed prior to the mechanistic framework imposed on science by men such as Newton, Galileo and Boyle. The organic elements existed in the thinking of Hermetic philosophers such as Campanella and Bruno in the seventeenth century, when the new science was being born. The Hermetic tradition became an important influence in the Renaissance of the latter part of the fifteenth century in Italy under the sponsorship of the Medici family. The organic tradition, which included Cabbalistic and Neoplatonic ideas as well as the Hermetic philosophy, rejected the mechanistic philosophy of the Greek atomists. There was more to the universe than matter in motion.

For them nature was 'alive' with sentience and qualities. They wrote of the world soul or *anima mundi* that 'informed' all material objects. They emphasised the intrinsic properties of physical things, including the property of self-motion. This was interpreted as an internal becoming, as contrasted with the motion of inert things, which was an external movement from one place to another in space (loco-motion from the Latin *locus*). Self-moving things have a degree of self-determination which inert objects do not have. These organic thinkers conceived of self-moving things as directly affecting one another, even when they were not in physical contact; they believed in action at a distance.

Far from being opposed to science, the organic tradition influenced scientists of note such as Copernicus, Kepler, Gilbert, Harvey and even Newton. Newton was deeply influenced by alchemy. The word alchemy is thought to have come from the Greek word for Egypt, the presumed home of the factitious Hermes Trismegistus, the supposed author of Hermetic philosophy. Contrary to the traditional view of the history of science, the organic tradition could be said to have been largely responsible for the rebirth of science (see, e.g., Kearney 1971; Klaaren 1977; Yates 1972). It emphasised the necessity of experiment rather than reliance on the authority of Aristotle. The organic view of nature was replete with aims and sympathies and deity as present in the world. It thus provided a unification of scientific and religious concerns. Some followers of the organic tradition had views that were magical and occult. Others were alchemists. So the tradition was quite varied in its details, as indeed is the mechanistic tradition.

However, the organic tradition was to become the rejected view. In its place the legalistic-mechanistic universe, with its elementary constituents of 'vacuous actualities', was established as the orthodoxy of science. It is called mechanistic because it develops the mechanistic materialism of the Greek atomists, especially Democritus. It is called legalistic in its view of nature because of the influence of the voluntarist theologians, Scotus, Ockham and the Protestant Reformers, especially Calvin. The term voluntarism refers to a God who wills (from the Latin *voluntarius*) certain events to happen. The order of nature is due to divinely imposed laws. The legalistic view of nature was emphasised by leading scientists such as Boyle and Newton and was given its imprimatur in no uncertain terms by Descartes when he wrote to Mersenne in 1630: 'God sets up mathematical laws in nature, as a king sets up laws in his kingdom'.

Emergence

The most common view amongst biologists as to the origin of consciousness is that it came into existence in mammals, possibly in birds and even possibly in all animals that have a central nervous system. Some (e.g., Donald Griffin 1981) extend the range of consciousness or something akin to it to Coelenterates (e.g., jellyfish), which have a nerve net, and perhaps to the single-celled Protozoa, because of the obvious responsiveness of these organisms to physical stimuli. The orthodox view amongst biologists is that consciousness came into existence at some stage of the evolution of animals. Prior to that stage there was no consciousness and no mind. Humans have minds but, many would say, frogs probably do not and jellyfish definitely not. The use of the word mind in this discussion is difficult because sometimes it is made to be synonymous with consciousness. Those who use it in this sense might say that a bee does not have a mind, though activities go on in the neurones in its brain. They would also say that these activities are purely physical and do not warrant the label of mind.

The doctrine of *emergence* was formulated by Lloyd Morgan (1923) in his book *Emergent Evolution*. According to Morgan, in the course of evolution there were a number of miracles that were interposed into the stream of evolutionary events. He recognised two as having special importance, the emergence of life and the emergence of mind. Their appearance were miracles in the sense that they were not to be understood and could not be understood in terms of physics and chemistry. Morgan believed that when life and later mind emerged in evolution, new laws besides those of physics and chemistry came into existence. This doctrine would hardly be of more than historic interest now except that the doctrine of emergence, shorn of the miracles posited by Morgan, is part of the framework of thought implicit, if not explicit, in the writings of many biologists. Dobzhansky (1967), for example, refers to the evolutionary appearance of life and mind as 'emergences or transcendences, in the evolutionary process' (p. 32). He made it clear that, in his view, something completely new came into existence when life came from the lifeless and mind came from the mindless. In this scheme, life and mind are exceptions to the whole of the rest of the evolutionary process in which everything had its precursor. In this discussion the question is not usually asked — Do conscious feelings arise from non-conscious ones? This question is discussed later in this chapter.

Emergence is a common doctrine in evolutionary thinking about the origin of organs. For example, no animals had feathers until birds appeared on the scene. Feathers are said to have emerged from something which were not feathers, namely the scales of reptiles. The five-toed limb is said to have emerged from fish that had no such limbs but fins. Analogously, minds are said to have emerged from something that had no mind. This is the orthodoxy of evolutionary thinking today. But this last step contains a serious flaw which is philosophically known as a *category mistake* (Griffin 1988, pp. 19, 147, 151; 1995).

Feathers, bones, eyes, ears, limbs and the rest of the organs of animals are externalistic properties knowable to sensory experience. But experience itself does not belong in this category. It is what an organism is for itself, not something that is observed through the eyes, ears, or hands of another organism. As David Griffin (1988) says: 'To put experience itself in the same class as those properties that are *objects* of experience is a *category mistake* of the most egregious kind' (p. 147). Likewise, some supporters of this view draw the analogy between what they call the emergence of mind with properties that have emerged in particular combinations of atoms, such as saltiness or wetness. Saltiness is a property of sodium chloride but not a property of either sodium (which is a metal) or chlorine (which is a gas), which together constitute sodium chloride. Wetness is a property of hydrogen and oxygen combined in the ratio H_2O but it is not a property of either of the gases hydrogen or oxygen. Likewise, it is argued, mind and experience have arisen out of a particular configuration of nerve cells, none of which by themself has mind or experience. To compare mind with saltiness and wetness is to commit the category mistake. Saltiness and wetness are properties of things as they appear to us from without. But, as David Griffin (1988) has said, 'conscious experience itself is not a property of things as they appear to us from without; it is what we are, in and for ourselves' (p. 19).

The confusion that leads to a category mistake is one that is common in the literature of science, yet this confusion is rarely recognised. Thomas Nagel (1979) makes the point when he says that 'much obscurity has been shed on the [mind-body] problem by faulty analogies between mental-physical relation and relations between the physical and other objective aspects of reality' (p. 83). He goes on to make the point that it is unintelligible to speak of the emergence of experience, which is something for itself, out of things that are purely physical.

Some philosophers are sceptical of making distinctions between so called categories on the grounds that they cannot agree as to what criteria are to be used to distinguish between categories. Yet surely one of the important procedures in philosophy is to make judgments as to which things are similar and which are dissimilar, and the degree of similarity. There is surely a difference in kind of a major sort between things one sees with one's eyes and that which is not visible but is experienced within. If these are not different categories, one wonders if any things are different.

There are two forms of the doctrine of emergence, a dualist and a physicalist form. A few scientists and philosophers hold a dualistic emergentism, once the mind emerges it is as a fully actual entity with the power to affect the body (e.g., Popper & Eccles 1977; Sperry 1992a, 1992b). Most scientists and philosophers hold a physicalist view of emergentism; 'mind' is just a property or aspect of the brain or some portion thereof, with no power to exert causation on the body. There are some physicalists who deny there is anything to emerge and therefore there is no need to continue to use subjective language (eliminative materialism).

Emergence implies that there was a point in biological evolution when mind emerged and the first sentient creatures came

into existence. Where then is the line to be drawn between the
sentient and the non-sentient? Descartes drew it between the
human soul and the rest of nature. But drawing an absolute line
anywhere is quite arbitrary, be it between humans and all others
or between fish and frogs. Some want to draw a line between living and non-living matter, but biologists now reject this as arbitrary. There is no clear line between a cell and a virus. Are then
the cell and virus sentient while their DNA and RNA macro-
molecules are not?

Reductionism

The materialist, physicalist or mechanical view of the universe is reductionist. Reductionists try to explain the
properties of complex wholes such as molecules or living
organisms in terms of the units of which those molecules and living organisms are composed. They would argue that the properties of a protein molecule could be determined and predicted in
terms of the properties of its atoms, electrons, protons, etc., as
studied by classical physics. Some reductionists argue that human
behaviour is to be understood solely in terms of chemistry. Yet the
phenomena of human behaviour are simultaneously biological
and social. An adequate explanation must include both. Steven
Rose (1995) argues against what he calls the rise of neurogenetic
determinism. This is a form of biological reductionism that attributes all human behaviour to genes and their effects on the brain.

> Although only the most extreme reductionist would suggest that
> we should seek the origins of the Bosnian war in deficiencies in
> serotonin-reuptake in Dr Karadzic's brain, and its cure by the
> mass prescription of Prozac, many of the arguments offered by
> neurogenetic determinism are not far removed from such
> extremes. Give the social its due, the claim runs, but in the last
> analysis the determinants are surely biological. And anyhow, we
> have some understanding and possibility of intervention into the
> biological, but rather little into the social (p. 380).

It is Rose's argument that such naive neurogenetic determinism is
based on faulty reductionism.

There is, however, a valid form of reductionism. Different

sciences investigate the world at different levels and the study at one level may be greatly helped by the study at a lower level. Thus at the level of the living organisms much can be understood in terms of the biochemistry of cells that constitute the organism. Biochemistry throws light on biology. Physics throws light on chemistry. The naive reductionist believes that biological phenomena will only be fully understood through molecular biology. Molecular biology then becomes the theophany of reductionism in biology. For a critique of this view see Lewontin (1991).

If complex things such as living organisms can be broken down into their component parts, how is it that the whole has properties that the components do not have? It is evident that the properties of the whole are not found in the parts, except as they are organised in that whole. It is for this reason that the reductionist program is deficient. One response has been to say that the whole is more than the sum of the parts. The tendency has been to interpret that in terms of the architectural arrangements of the parts. The properties of the patterned system will be different from the properties of the elements that constitute it. There is an element of truth in this statement, but it does not go far enough.

It is not just that the whole is more than the sum of its parts. It is that parts become qualitatively different by being parts of a whole. Yet few there be who seem to understand this critical distinction. A carbon atom in a diamond (which consists entirely of carbon atoms) has different properties from a carbon atom in an enzyme (which consists of many different sorts of atoms). But what could give it these different properties? The most fundamental answer to this question is in terms of the doctrine of internal relations and as Cobb (1984) has said, the most fundamental basis for rejecting reductionism as adequate to explain the physical world is the doctrine of internal relations (p. 151). Earlier Hartshorne (1934) had made much the same point when he said: 'Materialism overlooks...the internal relations involved in individuals' (p. 20).

According to the doctrine of internal relations, the relations of one entity to others are constitutive of the entity in question. The carbon atom in a diamond has relations to a multitude of carbon atoms around it. The carbon atom in an enzyme has relations to many different sorts of atoms in its environment. In each case the carbon atom is conceived to take into account internally those relations. It is not just a matter of architecture. The bricks that are built into an office block remain the same if that office block is torn down and the bricks are then built into a cathedral. The brick is not an individual entity but an aggregate of individual entities. One brick is not influenced in its being by the presence of another brick or a rock or anything else next to it in the building. Not so for an atom in a molecule or a molecule in a cell.

The properties of a system cannot be derived from the properties of the constituent parts, that is from the properties possessed by these entities when outside the system. A virus in a cell lacks certain properties it exhibits when in a cell. Molecules exhibit properties that cannot be derived from the properties of the atoms constituting them, when these atoms exist outside the molecular structure.

As Cobb (1984, p. 151) says, the effect of the doctrine of internal relations on the understanding of the nature of the physical world is radical. It destroys the notion of material substance and substitutes that of an event. The nature of the event is analogous to what we recognise as feeling in our own lives. This particular understanding of internal relations is derived from Whitehead (1942, Chapter 11). He also uses an alternative term 'prehensions' for internal relations.

I have already discussed the meaning of internal relations in human beings in Chapter 1. It is the subjective aspect of our lives, such as our feeling of courage or our feeling of redness, which feelings are not simply identical with the biochemical and physical processes that are involved in the physiology of such feelings. The objective of that chapter was to establish the reality of the subjective in humans, which cannot be reduced to nothing but the non-subjective such as chemical reactions. As is discussed in the section that follows the next one, the physical world is best understood not by reductionism alone but in addition by the interpretation of the lower levels in terms of the higher levels, which is from the perspective of our own human experience of internal relations.

Things that do not feel

The proposition of panexperientialism is that subjectivity (feeling in some form) exists in individual entities such as electrons, atoms, cells and organisms. There is no reason why we should not say that an electron is attracted to a proton. We mean then that the electron takes into account internally the proton in its environment. The proposition is that all entities such as electrons, cells and humans have internal relations. They can all be called organisms. The definition of an individual entity is that which acts and feels as one. When using the word feeling in relation to an electron we are not proposing that the electron is conscious. Feelings may be conscious, as in ourselves, or unconscious and presumably very attenuated, as in an electron. The word panexperientialism means the presence of experience in some form all the way down.

We know that protons and electrons and atoms and much more existed long before there were any humans to perceive them. And as Cobb (1995) proposes: 'They must have had reality in themselves, and that makes sense only if we affirm that they had reality for themselves. To have reality for itself an entity must feel' (p. 64). Or to put it another way we know from the physicist that electrons, protons and the like take account of their environment in a way that influences them. This internal relating we have called a primitive form of feeling or experience. From that it follows that to be real an entity must feel.

The doctrine of internal relations is akin to Teilhard de Chardin's concept of 'the within of things' as contrasted with the external appearance of things. A similar distinction is made by David Bohm in his distinction between the implicate order of nature and the explicate order. The latter is the order that physicists normally confine their attention to (see Birch 1990, pp. 79-80).

A distinction has to be made between individual entities such as electrons and protons and so-called compound individuals. A cell is a compound of individual entities such as atoms and molecules.

But not all things that exist are individual entities or compounds of them. A distinction has to be made between individual entities or their compounds and aggregates of individual entities such as chairs and planets. A chair has no internal relations. It is what it is whether it be in a school or a factory. Its being is quite independent of its environment. An aggregate is a grouping of entities that does not lead to a higher order of unified experience. The *pan* in panexperientialism means that all things either are experiences or are aggregates of individuals that are experiences. A molecule is an example of the first. A rock is an example of the second.

There is a variety of things that come under the definition of aggregates. A chair, a computer and a motor car are aggregates. They have each a considerable organisation but there is no evidence that they exhibit a unified experience. A pile of sand is an aggregate and so too is a rock of granite. The rock is far more organised than is a pile of sand, but there is no evidence that either has a unified experience. Panexperientialism asserts, not that all things have mind and feeling, but that all physical things are composed of individual entities (their atoms, etc.) that experience.

There is a whole group of organisms, such as plants and sponges, that are not compound individuals, that is individuals that have a unified experience. But they are so different from rocks and chairs that it does not seem appropriate to put them in the same category. They are highly organised and sustain that organisation while they are alive. In the case of plants, this maintenance is largely dependent upon the function of plant hormones. Whitehead suggested that we call these sorts of organisms 'living democracies'. The main point of this discussion is to emphasise that there are plenty of objects in the world that have no unified experience despite the high degree of their organisation. It is an important point because some critics of panexperientialism incorrectly accuse its proponents of supposing that rocks and solar systems have unified minds. They don't.

Panexperientialism generalises experience (feeling) to all individual entities (such as electrons) and compound individuals (such as cells). Consciousness is understood as a high-level experience. It involves memory of the past and anticipation of future events. At its highest level it involves richness of experience with its components of zest and harmony.

Science for the most part studies aggregates such as steel balls on inclined planes. When science studies individual entities, or their compounds, it does so as if they are aggregates, for science studies them as machines that have no internal relations. It is no exaggeration to say that most scientists simply do not know how to think about the world except as a machine. The study of things as if they are machines may be appropriate, depending upon the question that is being asked. For example, the mechanism of the heart is appropriately studied as a force pump. Likewise there are aspects of the physiology of the muscles and bones which are appropriately studied as levers. There seem to be aspects of the functioning of the brain which may have some parallels to computers. But I have argued that subjectivity has remained quite impervious to the mechanistic and reductionist approach.

The higher to lower as opposed to the lower to higher approach

Instead of putting all our eggs into the reductionist basket of analysis, the lower to higher approach, we can also make a higher to lower approach. We can put the principle of higher to lower approach in what, to some, is a startling proposition: *'Human experience is a high-level exemplification of reality in general'* (Cobb & Griffin 1976, p. 13). There is more in the saint than in the amoeba, and we shall gain a truer perspective of the whole process if we study it from its most recent results rather than only from its beginnings. Instead of looking at nature only from the bottom up, we look at nature also from the top down. That is the aspect of nature which we know most directly: our inner life of experience. We know that in a way in which we know nothing else. Why then should such information be ignored as we seek to interpret the nature of nature? But that is precisely what is done in the bottom-up approach. Classical biology sees all organisms as machines. Classical physics does the same with its particles. The alternative is to interpret all in the light of that aspect of reality that we know most intimately. That leads to a *panexperiential* view of nature. Far more entities are experiential than most of us recognise. But not all experience is conscious. The proposition is not that atoms and molecules are conscious but that there is at that level something akin to sentience which takes into account internally the environment. At higher levels, such as a human being, the internal relations become conscious. We can talk about a richness of experience that is different for a mosquito compared with a human being. So it is proper to speak of an evolution of experience which at some stage enters into consciousness. Beings with conscious experience evolved from forebears in which experience was not conscious.

The doctrine of internal relations has important implications for the scientific enterprise. That enterprise has for the most part been committed to the reductionist approach. Alongside reductionist analysis we need to study phenomena at each level as they are shaped by phenomena at a higher level. There is absolutely no reason why the whole world of inner experience should not be included in the domain of science. Brain physiologist Roger Sperry has said just this, recognising its implication that science can then speak of causation from higher to lower, exerted by events of inner experience. In other words, feelings and mind in whatever form are recognised as causes (Griffin 1990, p. 85).

The effect of the doctrine of internal relations on the understanding of nature is radical. As I have already said it destroys the notion of material *substance* and substitutes that of an *event*. The notion of substance is something that exists independently of anything else. The atoms of Democritus were substances. Classical physics implies that there are substances such as atoms and molecules that then behave in certain ways. In event, thinking events come first and are more basic. The world is made of events, not substances. A hydrogen atom is an event, so is every so-called fundamental particle such as a proton. Modern physics recognises this, though it still tends to use the language of substance thinking. The events that constitute the being of any atom or proton are their internal relations. An internal relation, unlike an external relation, is constitutive of the character, even the existence of something. The relation between internal relations and events is explored in more detail by Birch and Cobb (1981, pp. 84-91).

The central idea of this section is the proposition that we need to study phenomena at each level (such as the level of the atom) as they are shaped by phenomena at a higher level (such as a living person). I was first led to see the significance of this approach by reading Whitehead's *Science and the Modern World*. I was introduced to its relevance in biology by Australian W. E. Agar's (1943) book *A Contribution to the Theory of the Living Organism*. The very first sentence in this book reads: 'The main thesis of this book is that all living organisms are subjects...that the characteristic activity of a subject is the act of perception; and that perception is the establishment by the subject of its causal relation with the external world' (p. 7). Having given his reasons for this statement, he went on to develop Whitehead's concept that all of reality from protons to people is process. Hence the title of Whitehead's Gifford Lectures, *Process and Reality*. The process, moreover, is one of feeling or experience. So the ultimate entities of the world are not objects but subjects. For Whitehead, subjects are the final real things of which the world is made. There is no going behind them to find anything more real. 'If there were no subjects there would be nothing, nothing, bare nothing.'

The word feeling or experience for an elementary individual entity such as an electron or an atom, as well as for events in the mind of humans, is an example of the thoroughgoing unification of nature which Whitehead's system seeks to achieve. *Feeling or experience is used for any kind of acting or being acted upon in such a way that the make-up or constitution of the subject is affected.* Another way of putting this is to say that the entity takes account of its environment in such a way that it is itself constituted, at least in part, by that internal relationship. The analogy with human experience is complete. We are what we are by virtue of our internal relations, which change our constitution moment by moment and day by day. The poet Tennyson was correct when in 'Ulysses' he said: 'I am a part of all that I have met'.

There are difficulties in using the words feeling and experience for events that are not conscious because we usually associate these words with conscious activities. Yet it is extremely important to any understanding that we think of there being different degrees of consciousness shading off into unconsciousness.

Dreaming is a form of conscious experience which may never-theless grade into a semi-conscious state. In Chapter 1 I discussed evidence for unconscious mind in humans which in various cir-cumstances can become conscious mind. A great deal of mental activity goes on in our lives that is at the unconscious level. Indeed most of human experience is unconscious. So it should not be too great a jump in our thinking to begin to use the words experience and feeling for events that are not conscious as well as for events that reach the conscious state. It would be nice to have a word that includes both conscious and unconscious experience but there does not seem to be one in the English language. So we instead use the words feeling and experience in this sense.

Biological evolution in this perspective is seen not just as involving mechanical changes, say to the heart as a pump, but internal changes whereby the experience or internal relations become richer in a human as compared with a mosquito or an atom. This view overcomes the problem of the emergence of mind from no-mind and of living from non-living. There is no such emergence, at least in the sense in which this word is gener-ally used.

Nevertheless there is, in evolution, creation of novelty. A human experience is novel compared with the experience of a dinosaur. A world of dinosaurs without humans is a different world from one that contains humans. But human experience has a continuity in origin with the feelings that constituted the being of the first mammals, the reptiles from which they evolved and all individual entities prior to them in the evolutionary line leading to *Homo sapiens*.

We should oppose the idea that what 'emerges' in the course of evolution is *totally* novel. To do that is to fall into the error of dualism. Conscious mental states are very different from non-conscious mental states but they are not totally different. And there is no reason to say that non-conscious mental states are totally different from still more primitive modes of internally tak-ing account of the environment.

Before the insights of quantum physics became a part of our knowledge, one could have objected that the idea of entities such as electrons and atoms having an experiential side just did not tie in with physics. It did not fit with classical or so-called Newtonian physics. But now the story is different. The laws of classical mechanics are no longer applicable to very small-scale phenomena. The real significance of quantum physics, suggests Max Delbruck (1986), is that it forces us to view mind and matter as aspects of a single system. This is not the place to pursue that in detail. To some extent it forms the subject of discussion in Birch and Cobb (1981, pp. 130-4), Birch (1990) and Griffin (1990). The important point is that the new physics is totally consistent with the notion of internal relations. I would go further and say that it virtually demands some such concept.

The use of the words feeling and experience for a living cell is difficult for many people to comprehend. Even more so is the suggestion that these words can be applied to an elementary physical event such as an electronic vibration. But I would emphasise again that the word feeling in this context refers to the taking account of the environment in such a way that the electron is constituted by that taking into account. It must be a very complete taking into account if, as some quantum physicists claim, an electron at one end of the universe can be influenced instantaneously by an electron at the other end of the universe!

The argument that brings us to this position is fully consistent with the usual methods in science, as was clearly put by Agar (1943):

> The physical scientist does not hesitate to ascribe to atoms the properties he finds it necessary to ascribe to them in order to interpret the properties of matter on a larger scale. But atoms also compose brains. On the same principle therefore we should ascribe to atoms a property which will be consistent with their function as elements in the brain as a locus of mental activity. Surely the only property of atoms which could provide what we are looking for is some form of mental activity in themselves (p. 108).

A similar argument was put by J. S. Haldane who said 'That a meeting-place between biology and physical science may some time be found there is no reason for doubting. But we may confidently predict that if that meeting-place be found, and one of the two sciences is swallowed up, that one will not be biology' (quoted by Hardy 1965, p. 265). In another place J. S. Haldane (1935) wrote:

> We can only discern a little mind in a dog, and at present none in an oyster or an oak. Nevertheless...if we ever explain life and mind in terms of atoms, I think we shall have to attribute to the atoms the same nature as that of minds or constituents of mind such as sensations.

The classical physicist might want to argue that physics has got on very well, thank you, without ascribing to atoms and electrons anything subjective, so why introduce it at all at that level? Below a certain level of organisation it may not be necessary, for some of the purposes of physics, to take into account the mental aspects of the entities concerned. But that is no reason to assume its absence and then to have to suppose that it made its appearance out of the blue at some late date in the history of the universe. There is no need to believe in that sort of miracle.

It makes more sense to propose that the stuff of the world is mind-stuff. Writing in the 1930s physicist James Jeans said: 'The universe begins to look more like a great thought than like a great machine. Mind no longer appears as an accidental intruder in the realm of matter' (Barbour 1990, p. 114). Writing 60 years later physicist Paul Davies (1992) says: 'I have come to the point of view that mind — i.e., conscious awareness of the world — is not a meaningless and incidental quirk of nature, but an absolutely fundamental facet of reality' (p. 16). And in his book *The Mind Matters* David Hodgson (1991) says: 'It is more reasonable to believe that the mental and the rational has not emerged from the physical, but somehow has existed at least as long as the physical has existed (p. 458). Each of these writers is pointing a way out of the morass of materialism to a more feeling universe.

Prigogine and Stengers (1984) and Kauffman (1993) have analysed what are known as self-organising systems, in which disorder at one level leads to order at another. An example is the self-assembly of proteins that constitute the complex 'head, neck and tail' of a bacteriophage virus. It seems that the bringing together of one protein with another leads to an order in which other proteins are self-assembled to form the complex structure. It is a mistake to suppose that this self-organisation is analogous to a motor car making itself from its parts. It makes more sense to suppose that a protein is what it is and does by its taking account of other entities in its environment, such as other proteins. The constituent parts can be understood only in their relation to the whole organisation. This taking account of is a form of mind. This approach is usually the one left out of account. Yet it could be central to our understanding of nature at all levels.

Two contemporary philosophers have independently supported the proposition that experience in some form is an aspect of nature right down to the so-called fundamental particles. Chalmers (1995) points out how a remarkable number of phenomena have turned out to be explicable wholly in terms of entities simpler than themselves. But this is not universal. Occasionally in physics it happens that an entity has to be taken as *fundamental*. Fundamental entities are not explained in terms of anything simpler. They are taken as basic. For example, in the nineteenth century it turned out that electromagnetic processes could not be explained in terms of the wholly mechanical processes that previous physical theories appealed to, so Maxwell and others introduced electromagnetic charge and electromagnetic forces as new fundamental components of physical theory. Other features that physical theory takes as fundamental include mass and space-time. No attempt is made to explain these features in terms of anything simpler. Chalmers' proposition is that a theory of consciousness should take experience as fundamental alongside mass, charge and space-time. Of course taking experience as fundamental does not tell us why there is experience in the first place. But nothing in physics tells us why there is matter in the first place. This is just the way the world is.

Along similar lines to Chalmers' argument, Strawson (1994) starts off with the proposition that experience is a real aspect of our world, yet nothing in current physics covers the fact that entities experience. Therefore there must be physical properties of which physics is so far ignorant. He asks the question — What kind of physical theory might capture the nature of mental properties? His answer is — One that includes experience as fundamental. So Strawson, together with Chalmers and indeed with the process thought argued in this book, says that today's physics is radically incomplete when it fails to include any theory of one of the most salient and sure characteristics of reality, namely conscious experience. A genuinely unified physical theory would have to find a place for experience, linking it to other aspects of the physical world. Strawson points out that physics at present ignores consciousness, thereby dodging a problem it should try to explain.

David Griffin believes that we seem to be on the verge of a major revolution in the worldview associated with the natural sciences, comparable in scope with that of the seventeenth century. One of his reasons is the growing awareness that science does not require a completely mechanistic worldview. Much evidence suggests a more dynamic, less deterministic interpretation of nature. Another reason is a growing desire to have a worldview that makes our scientific viewpoint consistent with our own inner freedom and internal experience of the world (Griffin 1990, p. 89).

The panexperiential view of nature is an unprovable hypothesis; but so is the idea that low-grade entities do not have any form of experience. Each hypothesis can only be tested by examining the conclusions to which it leads. If panexperientialism is more adequate and self-consistent than either emergentism or physicalism, is that not a good reason for taking it seriously?

Conclusion

Concerning the origin of mind, there are three possibilities: mind arises from no-mind (the doctrine of emergence); there is no such entity as mind as distinct from matter (physicalism); or the stuff of all existence is mind-stuff (panexperientialism). The dominant views today are the doctrine of emergence and physicalism.

These three views have had a long history. Between the middle of the fifteenth century and the latter half of the seventeenth century various organismic views of nature, some of which had a panexperientialist view, held sway. These views were rejected with the rise of mechanistic science, which originally held the mechanistic view of nature within a dualist view that included souls and deity. When this dualism was rejected, however, the mechanistic view implied a doctrine of emergence. The physicalist view, which virtually rejects the notion of mind, goes back to Greeks such as Democritus and is held by some modern philosophers.

The dominant doctrine of the emergence of mind from no-mind commits a *category mistake* of likening the emergence of mind in animals from organisms that had no minds to the emergence of feathers in birds from scales in reptiles.

The view here propounded is that mind cannot arise from no-mind and that no line can be drawn between sentient entities such as animals and entities such as molecules, atoms and electrons. The difference is a difference in degree, not in kind. But the difference in degree makes all the difference.

The overriding principle of panexperientialism is that human experience is a high-level exemplification of reality in general. The stuff of the world is mind-stuff. The recognition of a less deterministic view of nature and of internal relations of individual entities constitutes a revolution in worldview comparable in scope with that of the scientific revolution of the sixteenth and seventeenth century.

4

The Myth of the Computer

I want to put the final nail in the coffin of the theory that the mind is a computer program. And I want to make some proposals for reforming the study of mental phenomena in a way that would justify the hope of rediscovering the mind.

JOHN SEARLE (1992, p. XI)

Minds with their thoughts and feelings are computer programs, no more, no less. That is the proposition of 'strong artificial intelligence' (strong AI). The proposition is that what we call minds are very complex digital computer programs. Mental states are computer states and mental processes are computational processes (e.g., Dennett 1991). Mental states have no special connection with nerves and brains, so the argument goes. It just so happens that the brain is a computer made of nerve cells, but there are other sorts of computers that use chips instead of nerve cells. Proponents of strong AI claim that their computers think and they anticipate that one day they will have a computer that does just about all the brain can do. Hence the caption 'The search for machines with a soul' that headed a review of a recent book on the history of the search for artificial intelligence. It could indeed be said that the faith of strong AI is the theophany of materialism.

To simulate what the brain does is an awesome project. The human brain contains at least 10 billion nerve cells. Each nerve cell has about a thousand points of connection (dendrites) to neighbouring cells. This allows for the possibility of about a million billion interconnections to other nerve cells. This number is more than the number of electrons in the universe! A matchhead's worth of the brain contains about a billion connections. At the speed with which information travels in the system there are around ten thousand billion connections per second. The entire world telephone system — the most complex machine on Earth — carries less than a billion calls each year. Computers are not going to match human brains for a long time to come.

When one contemplates the miriad of nerve cells and their manifold connections, together with some 3000 different biochemical compounds in the brain identified to date, one can begin to grasp the stupendous complexity of this, the most complex object in the universe. Somehow, in ways as yet unknown, consciousness arises from the enormously complex interactions of the billions of nerve cells in the brain.

The mammoth Cyc computer system is planned to have ten million interconnected bits of information keyed into the data base. It is a $25 million program that encompasses 200 person-years' effort. It will store a colossal number of basic bits of information such as 'people come in two kinds, men and women'. Undoubtedly, the bigger and the faster the computer, the more success there will be in accessing and using this knowledge. It is hoped that this will have enough basic information to perform everyday tasks such as controlling a robot to clean the house (Davidson 1993).

Some advocates of AI argue as if storing all the encyclopaedias of the world in a computer would result in a super-wise machine. A knowledgeable machine such may be, but one that is better able to add wisdom to, say, the debate on a new international order — no. That kind of creativity is not contained in encyclopaedic knowledge but requires leaps of insight which, as yet, no expert system has achieved. The advocates of strong AI anticipate that one day a computer will be constructed out of chips that will have all the requisite properties of brains and much more besides. It is proposed that such computers will both think and feel. How would you know when a computer possessed these mental states?

The Turing test

For advocates of AI the Turing test is the criterion of mental states. When Alan Turing, who was a pioneer in the 1930s and '40s, got tired of addressing the question 'Can machines think?' he shifted the debate. Since thinking is hard to define, he said the real issue is whether a machine can carry on a conversation with a person in such a way that the person cannot tell whether he is talking to a machine or a person. 'Turing tests', in which volunteers converse via keyboards and monitors with specially programmed computers, have already been carried out, but as yet no machine has succeeded in fooling its human interlocutors. Professor Marvin Minsky, one of the major contributors to AI, believes he achieves this goal in a novel with co-author Harry Harrison. The novel is called *The Turing Option* (Harrison & Minsky 1992). The brilliant young prodigy of the novel invents a machine called Sven. It learns so fast that soon its conversation is almost indistinguishable from that of its maker.

However, even Sven seems unable to think for itself, which is surely the point of Turing's challenge.

It is not particularly challenging that a computer can outperform even the best mathematician. That has no more significance than the fact that a steam shovel can outperform the best human digger. A computer can be made to play chess with a clever chess player. It is given accurate information in its program about possible moves and is given perfect information about the other's position and moves at any moment. There is no reason, in principle, why in the next ten years a computer program will not be able to outperform any human chess player. It can scan millions of possible positions, unlike any human chess player. But that fact is no more relevant to the issue of conscious mental events than is the fact that any pocket calculator can calculate faster than any human mathematician. The day that an AI program beats the world chess champion will make the computer about as interesting as the man on a bicycle in the Sydney to Surf footrace. Furthermore, chess is a game that is so constrained that it requires a very special form of intellectual ability. Away from the chessboard, the chess master is no more able to cope with the problems of life than the amateur. So while chess champions win victories, the machinery may not be able to make commonsense decisions.

As far as performance is concerned, we should, in principle, be able to build computers that exceed human performance in many kinds of activities. Already robots have helped to carry out hip replacements in California, prostate operations in London and brain surgery in Grenoble in France. Robodoc is the world's largest medical robot. In the half year November 1992 to June 1993, ten patients at Sutter General Hospital in Sacramento had hip replacements done with the aid of Robodoc. It is programmed to carve a cavity for an implant in the thigh bone. Why should a patient trust a robotic surgeon rather than the skilled hands of a human specialist? The most important reason is that an electronic arm is capable of precision well beyond that of the steadiest and best trained surgeon (Cookson 1993).

The principle of the robot is well illustrated by Sharkey, a robot invented in the late 1960s by Nils Nilsson and his colleagues at Stanford Research Institute in California. As described by Dennett (1991), Sharkey is a box with motorised wheels and a television camera for eyes. Conceived in the early days of electronic miniaturisation, Sharkey had a brain that was too big to keep on board, so the robot used a radio transmitter to communicate with a central computer. Human operators would type commands on a keyboard such as 'push the box off the platform'. Sharkey would dutifully explore the room until it found the box. Then it would push a ramp up to the platform, roll up on top and shove the box onto the floor. The robot was able to navigate because its software was designed to recognise the signature that boxes, pyramids and other objects left on the electronic retina of its video eye. As an object came into sight the computer would measure the differences in illumination, detecting an edge here, a corner there. Referring to rules about how different objects look from different vantage points, it might decide whether it was seeing, say, the slope of a pyramid or the incline of a ramp. The robot's brain was just processing signals, the ones and zeros of binary code.

The rules built into Sharkey are in principle the same as those in the most sophisticated robot of today such as WABOT-2, built by Ichiro Kato and his colleagues at Waseda University, Tokyo. WABOT-2 can recognise music, both heard and seen, and play the piano to concert standard. Its 80 or so microprocessors can solve the specific problem of learning music. Even more complicated in conception is Cog, a robot being made at the Massachusetts Institute of Technology. The project is to make it interact with people, such as playing with toys, passing things back and forth, stacking objects, all very similar actions to the activities of a baby (Lewin 1994).

Philosopher and psychologist Margaret Boden (1990) is quite sure that the brain is a kind of computer and that a computer can be programmed to mimic the sort of intelligence that could be called creative. As an example she quotes Aaron, which is a program consisting of a few hundred rules regarding artistic style. Each drawing generated by Aaron is a surprise to its inventor, the human artist Harold Cohen. Even though he wrote every line of the computer code he couldn't possibly anticipate all the permutations in which the code could be copied. Likewise, a composer of music works with a network of constraints (the principle of harmony) exploring combinations, much as Aaron explored the maze of all possible drawings that can be made with programmed rules. A computer program can simulate the constraints of harmony and explore possible components such as the jazz improviser written by Philip Johnson-Laird. It performs at the level of a moderately competent beginner. Levels of loudness, crescendos, rallentandos and the like can be built into the program for expression. Boden (1990) argues that these explorations with computer programs help us to understand the nature of creative artistic effort and should themselves be called creative.

As an aside to the discussion of the capabilities of computers, scientist Lord Bowden is recorded as having said that there seemed to be little point in spending vast sums of money on creating a computer as intelligent as a human when the world was already heavily overpopulated with intelligent beings, all of whom could be created quite easily, relatively cheaply and in a far more enjoyable way (Hodgson 1992, p. 83). Furthermore the capacity of a machine to do jobs that humans can do, and better, is not particularly relevant to the argument about what constitutes mind and consciousness.

But let's return to the Turing test. Is it really a valid test for determining whether a machine has mental states or not? John Searle (1992) argues convincingly enough, at least for me, that it is not. The reason is that the computer has syntax but no semantics. Syntax refers to the rules for putting words and sentences together. Semantics is the meaning of words and sentences. The computer manipulates formal symbols but attaches no meaning to them. Searle illustrates the point by means of his famous Chinese room analogy. Suppose I, who understand no Chinese at all and can't distinguish Chinese symbols from any other kind of symbols, am locked in a room with a number of boxes full of Chinese symbols. Suppose I am given a book of rules in English that instructs me how to match these Chinese symbols with each other. The rules say such things as that the 'squiggle-squiggle' sign is to be followed by the 'squoggle-squoggle' sign. Suppose that people outside the room pass in more Chinese symbols and that following the instructions in the book I pass symbols back to them. Suppose that unknown to me the people who pass me the symbols call them 'questions', and the book I work from they call 'the program' and me they call 'the computer.' Suppose that after a while the programmers get so good at writing the program and I get so good at manipulating the symbols that my answers are indistinguishable from those of native Chinese speakers. It passes the Turing test for understanding Chinese! Yet I do not understand a word of Chinese, and neither does any other computer because all the computer does is transform inputs into some sort of output without having any understanding of the meaning of the symbols. It attaches no meaning, interpretation, or content to any of the symbols. It has the syntax but not the semantics. The computer works with syntax (rules) but it has no understanding of what is going on. It follows that the way the brain produces conscious mental events cannot be solved by virtue of implementing formal computer programs. Something else must be going on in the brain.

The analogy of the Chinese room illustrates that strong AI commits what A. N. Whitehead (1933, pp. 64, 72) called 'the fallacy of misplaced concreteness.' In this case it identifies the mechanics of the workings of the brain with the concrete reality of experiencing, feeling and understanding. The model is an abstraction from reality. It is to mistake the map for the territory.

Searle (1992) argues that what works for Chinese works for other mental experiences. I could, for example, go through the steps of a formal program in my computer that simulates thirst. It might even be programmed to read out 'I am thirsty' or 'please give me a drink'. But would anyone suggest that we have the slightest reason to suppose that the computer is literally thirsty? Or that any sensation such as feeling depressed or understanding a story is a real sensation for the computer? The argument of the Chinese room refutes the Turing test because it shows that a system could pass the Turing test without having the appropriate mental states.

A computer program can simulate the formal properties of the sequence of chemical and electrical phenomena in the production of thirst, just as it can simulate hurricanes, internal combustion engines or the flow of currency in a depressed economy. But no one imagines that a computer simulation of an internal combustion engine will power a car or that simulation of a thunderstorm will produce one. To suppose that a computer program really simulates the brain is to confuse the abstraction of the mechanics of the brain's workings with the concrete reality of feeling thirsty. Again it is to commit the fallacy of misplaced concreteness. A computer might be made that could answer either yes or no to the question — Are bacon and tomato sandwiches sold in department stores? But in answer to the question—Are bacon and tomato sandwiches tasty? the appropriate machine might respond 'yes' or 'no' or 'don't know'. If the response is 'yes they are tasty', it nevertheless knows nothing about what to be tasty means. It has no experience of eating sandwiches.

The fallacy of misplaced concreteness inherent in much discussion about the capacities of computers fails to make the distinction between the mechanics of the brain and our experience of feeling. Nor is the mechanics of digestion the process of digestion. One might get the right pattern in the computer to match the pattern of stimuli-and-response in the stomach together with the right sequence of digestive enzymes, but that computer will not digest bacon and tomato sandwiches.

Searle's Chinese room argument is given in detail in his article (Searle 1980), along with 27 responses and a reply to the responses in the same journal. More responses by his critics are given in Lepore and van Gulick (1991). His up-to-date validation of his arguments in the light of all these criticisms can be found in Searle (1992). In the face of his critics his original arguments hold up well.

Information and understanding

Much of our knowledge and our feelings is more than an input of information that can be coded in words fed to a machine. Joseph Weizenbaum pointed this out in his critique of AI using the message 'Am arriving 7 o'clock plane, love, Bill'. This has a different information content for Bill's wife, who knew he was coming home, but not on precisely what plane, than for a woman who wasn't expecting Bill at all and who is surprised by his declaration of love. The information-content of a message is not a function of the message alone. It depends on the state of knowledge and the expectations of the receiver (Weizenbaum 1976, p. 209). When the boy touches the hand of the girl he loves, something is conveyed to her that cannot be equally conveyed in a symbolic representation in words, though the poet may do his best to find words to fill the gap.

Weizenbaum pointed out that because of our biological nature we have sensations to do with hunger, sex and the desire to love and to be loved. Their roots in some respects go back to their role in evolutionary survival. No computer would have any need for them. At most it might exhibit a desire for the nearest electric plug. No matter how successful we might be in simulating these emotions on a computer, the program would still be a simulation, not the real thing. Likewise David Gelernter (1994) tells us that someone might say to a computer 'I've lost my job' and the computer might be programmed to respond 'I understand'. But this reply is false, unless it can in some way feel the appropriate emotions engendered in the dismissed employee. It cannot empathise.

We know that mental states are produced by the brain. We know from the Chinese room argument that digital computer programs by themselves do not prove the existence of mental states. Now since brains do produce mental states, including sensations, and since programs by themselves cannot do this, it follows that the way the brain does it cannot be by simply installing a computer program. It follows that if you want to produce a machine that produces mental states, a thinking machine, you could not do it solely by having a certain kind of computer program. It would have to duplicate the specific causal powers of the brain, whatever they are. One is that certain stimuli passing to the brain result in sensations. Another is that in addition to syntax the human brain has semantic capacities. That is to say, sentences in the head give meanings, though semantic capacities are not part of the capacity of non-linguistic animals which yet are conscious (see Chapter 2). These propositions are in opposition to the materialist picture that mental phenomena — thoughts, feelings, sensations, desires, etc. — are nothing but computational events. On the other hand these considerations support the proposition that the activities of the brain are more than physics and chemistry and computer programs and contain an ineliminable subjective element. The nature of the subjective is discussed in Chapter 3.

Could a computer have feelings?

Might a computer be invented one day that has feelings? Just as was argued in Chapter 2 about non-human animals, a distinction has to be made between intelligent activities and consciousness. That a computer performs intelligent activities does not in itself tell us that it is conscious. While the exponents of AI have produced some clever problem-solving computer programs and have made some elementary robots that perform intelligent acts, it is now quite clear that if the brain is like a computer, it is not like a computer anyone has yet designed. But is it conceivable that some day such a brain-like computer might be invented? Let us suppose that if we could build with transistors or wires or whatever hardware an exact copy of the network of neurones in the human brain with its billions of connections and then set the electronic currents flowing in it, as they are now flowing in my brain, could that machine have written this sentence, got bored or excited, and could it contemplate its own existence?

Neurophysiologist Gerald Edelman (1992) builds models of the brain based on his understanding of how the brain works. He sees that the major error in AI is its tendency to ignore the biology underlying the mechanisms it purports to explain and, secondly, it has evaded 'the mystery of subjectivity'. It is an error, he argues, as dramatic as that of the model of the solar system before Copernicus put the sun at the centre. This failure is symptomatic of the failure of science to take account of the subjective as well as the objective. It is, he says, '*the* crisis in modern science'.

Edelman's is a complex theory which includes the idea that the 'wiring' of the brain, that is to say the neural connections, are worked out during the development of the brain and continue to change during experience. Those particular networks that work to the advantage of the creature are retained while others are lost or selected out. Memory in computers, for example, depends on the specifications and storage of bits of coded information. This is not the case in the nervous system of the brain. Memory in living organisms, by contrast, takes place through a much more dynamic system involving different neural connections in different contexts. This mechanism can now be simulated in artificial neural networks which is a step toward making a more biological-like brain in a computer.

Furthermore, perception is more complex and dynamic than its analogue in existing computers. For example, when pigeons are presented with photographs of trees, or oak leaves, or fish, surrounded by extraneous features, they rapidly learn to 'home in' upon these so that they can thereafter recognise any trees or oak leaves or fish straight away, however distracting or confusing the context may be. Artificial neural networks are now being explored that might make such pattern recognition.

Unlike other models of the brain, Edelman's is based on his theories of the mind and on the biological reality of the nervous system, in so far as this is known. On the basis of his theory of the brain, Edelman and his colleagues are constructing 'synthetic animals' which make use of super computers. He thinks that one day it might be possible to construct, in this way, a conscious 'artificial animal'. But he does not tell us how he would know if his robot was conscious. It is not enough to say — We would know when we see it. Lots of biologists and philosophers see bees. But they still dispute whether or not a bee is conscious. A distinction needs to be made between intelligent activity and conscious activity. Many robots perform intelligent activities and may do so better than humans. That suggests the possibility of their being conscious, but it in no way demonstrates that they are conscious. We would need further evidence to come to that conclusion. The argument is similar to that discussed in Chapter 2 as to whether non-human animals are conscious. There I gave six lines of evidence suggesting that non-human animals are conscious. One of them had to do with the similarity of their physiology and bio-chemistry to ours. Another has to do with their similar evolutionary history to ours. The point that applies to both computers and animals is that their display of intelligent behaviour in itself is not a demonstration that they are conscious.

The artificial brain, that Edelman hopes to construct, has no physiology and no biochemistry. It will still be a machine and not an organism in any real sense. The parts are not organisms like cells in the brain and so the total complex computer is an aggregate and not an individual entity. Aggregates like rocks or vacuum cleaners or computers have lots of properties but they do not have the property of having a unified experience. The human brain has a long evolutionary history of being built from the elaboration of individual entities that act and 'feel' as one: atoms, molecules, cells and so on. At each stage these individual entities, each one being more complex than its predecessor, are never just aggregates (see Chapter 3 for a discussion of aggregates). The ultimate units making up brains and computers (atoms and molecules) have their own primitive 'feelings'. The question is, can an aggregate of such entities (as in a computer) generate a unified feeling subject? It cannot. This is a factual judgment. There is no evidence that aggregates such as tables, solar systems and computers have unified feelings.

The proponents of strong AI would presumably argue that at some stage in the evolution of the complexity of the brain, mind emerges from no-mind. A miracle occurs. But as I argue in Chapter 3, the proposition that mind emerges from no-mind is an impossible one to sustain. It is based on the false assumption that the real world has no subjective component. It is more reasonable to propose that it has both subjective and objective aspects and that these two aspects have existed as long as anything has existed ,than to suppose that the subjective has emerged from the non-subjective or that it does not exist at all.

All these considerations touch not only on the capacities and limitations of computers, but also on the central questions of what it means to be a human being or any other sensate creature as well as what it means to be a computer. We come back again to the critical distinction between aggregates of individual entities that cannot act and feel as one and compound individual entities that do act and feel as one.

There are these two sorts of things in the world which cannot be reduced to the same thing. Rocks and vacuum cleaners and computers are fundamentally different from atoms, molecules, cells and animals. The law is that organisms that act and feel as one evolved from simpler organisms that act and feel as one. If that brings us back to the time before the first cell existed, the principle still holds. The first cell was a compound individual of molecules, which in their turn were compounds of atoms, and so on back to wherever cosmology leads us. But we shall never, in this view, be led back to a time when all was 'mere matter' with no subjectivity whatsoever. Ours is a universe of matter-mind. To think otherwise is to commit the matter-myth fallacy that mind emerged from no-mind.

Conclusion

The proposition of strong artificial intelligence (AI) is that minds are complex digital computer programs that should therefore be able to be replicated on computers. Mental states are equated with computational processes. So proponents of strong AI claim that present-day computers have mental states that include thinking and, if not yet, then in due course, feeling as well.

The so-called Turing test has been put forward as a test as to whether or not computers have mental states. There are, however, arguments that this is no test of mental states. A computer works with syntax (rules) but has no understanding (semantic capacities) of what is going on.

Instead of trying to simulate a brain by making more and more complex computers, there is a proposal to design a computer that is based on an understanding of how the brain works. As yet this program is in its infancy. However, such an artificial brain will still be a machine and not an organism in any real sense. The parts are not organisms like cells in the brain, so the computer is an aggregate and not an individual entity. The proposition of process thought is that only individual entities, or their compounds, have unified feelings. Aggregates, such as chairs and computers, do not. The brain has evolved over a long period of time as an elaboration of individual entities that act and feel as one. It is because these entities are experiential that the whole is also experiential. The mind of the brain is dependent upon the minds of its parts. The parts of computers are aggregates of atoms and molecules. But aggregates, by definition, do not have feelings.

5

God's Feelings

*I always think that when one feels one's been carrying a theory
too far, then's the time to carry it a little further. A little? Good
Heaven's, man! Are you growing old?*

MAX BEERBOHM, QUOTED IN REY (1993, p. 240)

This is a highly speculative chapter, but a necessary one for the complete story. Previous chapters have emphasised that we live in a feeling universe in the sense that the word feeling is appropriately applied to all individual entities of existence from protons to people. Of course the word feeling at the level of protons does not mean conscious feeling, but some element of subjectivity that is not conscious. We now ask — What is the origin of this subjectivity in nature? This question is insuperably difficult for mechanists who reduce all to machinery. There is no room in the mechanistic account for subjectivity, yet mechanists have to ask how the illusion arose since they know subjectivity in themselves — after all they do have feelings!

Amongst scientists, the question of the origin of subjectivity is more likely to be asked by biologists. That is the case in the thought of the developmental biologist C. H. Waddington, the geneticists Sewall Wright and Th. Dobzhansky and the zoologist W. E. Agar, whose book *A Contribution to the Theory of the Living Organism* I discuss in Chapter 3. Dobzhansky is quite explicit about relating the origin of subjectivity to a concept of God. Waddington and Sewall Wright are less so, except in private conversation. Agar (1951) concluded his book with the statement: 'It is indeed natural to see in the purposiveness of finite agents a manifestation of a cosmic teleology' (p. 225). But he adds that a discussion of such an agent is beyond the scope of his book, which was on the nature of the living organism. However, it is not beyond the scope of my book, speculative indeed as any answer to the problem may be. So it is time now to carry the argument about mind and consciousness a step further.

As far back in history that the physicist can take us is the 'big bang'. Not much existed then. But what existed then had the potentiality of becoming the universe as we know it today with our Earth inhabited by living organisms including us. Within that context Whitehead (1978) argued that 'the general potentiality of the universe must be somewhere' (p. 46). By general potentiality he meant as yet unrealised possibilities, values and purposes that are in some sense 'felt' by the individual entities of creation. By somewhere Whitehead meant 'some actual entity'. Whitehead named this actual entity the mind of God.

The proposition that the universal existence of subjectivity requires the existence of a cosmic mind at the heart of the universe is the subject of this chapter.

There are those who object to giving the word God this meaning. Their reason is that the word God is strongly tied to the supernatural God of a mechanistic universe, the omnipotent creator who gave the universe a kick start and then left it to run itself, with occasional interventions in the form of miracles. Because the traditional notion of God is tied to such ideas, Whitehead was reluctant at one stage to use the same word for the cosmic mind. However, the last chapter in his greatest work, *Process and Reality*, is entitled 'God and the World'. The God of that world is not the traditional omnipotent creator who manipulates things. God is different from that image, as we shall see.

The mind of God and the heart of God

P hysicist Paul Davies (1992) wrote a book called *The Mind of God*. Much of his book builds up a case for the existence of the laws of physics before there was any physical universe. The laws of physics, he says, are eternal and omnipotent. Some thinkers have argued that the laws of physics came into being with the universe. But then those laws cannot explain the origin of the universe, because the laws would not exist until the universe existed. It is as though the cosmic 'software' existed without the 'hardware'. Where then did the laws of physics exist? After nearly 200 pages Paul Davies suggests — in the mind of God. God is a mathematician.

The French mathematician and philosopher of the seventeenth century, Pascal, made the distinction between the God of the philosophers and the 'God of Abraham, Isaac and Jacob'. Paul Davies (1992) is quite forthright about this distinction also when he says: 'Nor is it obvious to me that this postulated being who underpins the rationality of the world bears much relation to the personal God of religion, still less to the God of the Bible or the Koran' (p. 191). Doubtless Abraham, Isaac and Jacob were unaware of the mathematical attributes of the philosopher-physicist's God. But that is not to say that anything about their idea of God ruled out such attributes, as Davies finds in his analysis. However, Pascal's distinction and Davies' apparent agreement with it lead me to pursue another side of the possible nature of God. And perhaps it is not surprising, my being a biologist, that I call this side the heart of God. I am not the first person to use the expression the heart of God. The word heart has been used creatively by Rita Brock (1988) to refer not to the divine but rather to the self that is internally related to the divine.

Jay McDaniel (1989) goes further and suggests reasons why the word heart is an appropriate metaphor for the divine itself:

> Heart is used to refer to inner feelings of sympathy, understanding, compassion, and care. We speak of people being 'full of heart' and by this we mean they have deep love and affection for others. For process thinkers the divine mystery is heartful in this sense in two ways. The cosmic Heart is active in the world as an inwardly felt lure, which is one way its love is expressed. It is also receptive of the world as an all-empathic consciousness, which is the other way its love is realised...Heart is the ultimate expression of relational power (pp. 143-4).

McDaniel points to other meanings of heart which he thinks make it an appropriate metaphor for the divine, such for example as 'centre of vital functions', 'innermost being' and 'centre of our lives'. The metaphor heart of God emphasises Pascal's personal 'God of Abraham, Isaac and Jacob'.

There is a stream of theistic thought in which God is not conceived as the omnipotent, supernatural, legalistic ruler of the universe. The ideas associated with omnipotence, intervention and law-giver are not part of process thought that underlies this book. Concepts of persuasive love, ultimate concern and infinite passion are. So why restrict the name God exclusively to a concept that is the antithesis of this view? Both streams of thought exist in the Judeo-Christian tradition and there are those of us who would claim that the emphasis on God as persuasive love as opposed to coercive power is central to the message of Jesus. What then is the nature of God as persuasive love? I suggest three propositions.

The feelings of God for the world

The first proposition is: *God acts in the world by compassionate persuasive love.*

I have described the subjective nature of individual entities from protons to people as having to do with feelings; the fundamental principle is that human experience is a high-level exemplification of reality in general. The word feeling is used in the sense of taking account of the environment internally such that the entity is constituted by that relationship. That is the nature of human friendship. At lower levels of organisation, feelings so defined are not conscious.

A subjective aspect of the relations of all individual entities, from protons to people, follows logically if subjectivity didn't come into existence towards the end of cosmic evolution but was a part of the process from the beginning. That all individual entities from protons to people have an inner reality as well as an outer one, that Teilhard de Chardin called the 'within of things', is in keeping with the human experience of the sense of kinship with all things. Although many people have lost this sense of kinship today, it has been a feature of human sensibility in most cultures at most times and places. So in reflecting upon our time Caroline Merchant (1980) writes of *The Death of Nature* and Rupert Sheldrake (1990) writes hopefully on *The Rebirth of Nature*. It is not that nature died and has to be reborn, but that our concept of a dead nature needs revivifying.

God acts by being felt by God's creatures, the individual entities of creation. God's envisagement of possibilities elicits a response from the individual entities of creation. A note on a tuning fork can elicit a response from a piano because the piano already has in it a string tuned to the same note. So it is with God and the individual entities of creation. God acts in human life by being felt by us as persuasive love that is transforming. 'In every event we are addressed by God,' said Martin Buber. We are tuned to tune in to the lure of God. The relationship is an internal relation. So it is with the rest of creation. When God is felt by the individual entities, God enters into their constitution. In this view, if God were withdrawn from the world the world would collapse. This aspect of God can be called the divine eros. The word eros is used to emphasise that this is a strongly felt relationship. God is lure, God is persuasive love, ever confronting the world as it now is with the possibilities of its future.

So it is true to say that the realm of possibility is in God. For our conscious lives the possibilities are values. Values are structured in the sense of having a gradation. At any particular moment only some values will be relevant. At the time of *Australopithecus,* a direct precursor of humans a million or so years ago, the realm of values relevant in the day to day life of this creature would have been restricted, compared to what is relevant for us. When humans began to form human societies, maybe a quarter of a millennium ago, the social possibilities were greater, yet limited, and so were the values that a society could make real. There is a fullness of time for every set of values that, until then, have been only possibilities not yet concretely real. The life and mission of Jesus would not have been possible except in a society that, through its history, had reached a certain critical point. In the fullness of time he was able to show men and women what human life could be. God confronts what is actual in the world with what is possible for it. This is the compassion of God for the creation.

Think back to the origin of the universe. Out of the depths of undifferentiated chaos, all the multitudinous forms of existence are going to be beckoned into being by call and response. A few seconds or whatever after the big bang the first of these forms was hydrogen. Nothing else existed in the universe. What then of the possibilities of God for becoming actual in the world? They were very limited at that moment until further steps were completed. There are, at any one moment, limitations to the possibilities of the future being actualised right at that moment. Yet the concept is that in God, even then, were inherent all the future possibilities of the universe. God contains the potentiality of the future.

This potentiality is not in the form of a blueprint of the future. Therefore it is misleading to speak of a divine design. The term design has the connotation of a preconceived pattern. The term divine purpose is better, as it does not carry this connotation. Nothing is completely determined. The future is open-ended.

One reason for this is that God is not the sole cause of all happenings. God exercises causality always in relation to beings who have their own measure of self-determination. The relationships become more complex obviously as the universe becomes more complex, when instead of just one sort of atom, hydrogen, there are many sorts of atoms and a multitude of creative individual entities ranging from atoms to people.

God acts by being and by having purposes. God's being is forever active. Whitehead speaks of the 'appetition' of God as the basis of all order. By appetition he means the appetite toward the realisation of what is not yet, but could be. Whitehead also says that the world lives by its incarnation of God in itself. These are images of an organic relation of God to the world.

This is the way in which the providence of God can be conceived. Providence is a difficult word with a number of meanings. The meaning in the present context is that God provides the possibilities. God is ever active and never needs to be persuaded to act.

Providence does not mean a divine planning by which everything is predetermined, as in an efficient machine. It means rather that there is a creative and saving possibility in every situation which cannot be destroyed by any event (Tillich 1953, p. 106). The *creative good*, which is God, works against obstacles and evils of all sorts. *Created goods*, and even creativity of various types, is often obliterated by the wickedness of human beings. But no evil can destroy creativity as such. It can be obstructed. The goods that have been created can be destroyed. But the process of creative good can begin again and construct again to higher levels. *Created goods* may perish but *creative good* is imperishable.

Plato was justified in saying: 'The creation of the world — that is to say, the world of civilised order — is the victory of persuasion over force'. We have reason to believe that the persuasive elements in life will forever maintain a precarious existence amidst the formidable march of ruthless powers. Has it ever been otherwise? The problem for us is that we do not discount the significance of the tender elements of existence that are more precious and more lasting than the staggering forces of destruction. The head however bloodied, and the heart however broken, may win from the struggles of life, and put back into the making of the world, certain spiritual values which make life glorious to live, despite the agony and the waste.

I am often asked by Christians, even a bishop on one occasion, of a traditional persuasion, why cannot God be both persuasive love yet also act coercively from time to time when necessary. The Holocaust would seem to be such a time. But did God stop the Holocaust and the suffering of six million Jews? The Christian of a traditional persuasion has no answer to that. If God could have prevented the Holocaust, yet chose not to, then by any definition, that God is malevolent. Would earthly parents stand by and watch while their child was killed by a madman? Such parents would be guilty. It is for this same reason that the evil and suffering in the world become the rock on which fundamentalist religion is shipwrecked.

Let me state as sharply as I can that God's use of persuasion is not based on a voluntary self-limitation. The idea that God's power is self-limited makes no sense at all. Let's be completely frank about that. There is absolutely no evidence for such a concept. God cannot choose from time to time to interfere coercively here and there at will. This is at the heart of the difference between classical theism and panentheism or neo-classical theism. God does not put up special umbrellas to protect the faithful against this or that special disaster, nor does God authorise any particular disaster. Oliver Cromwell sat up with his friends seeking divine guidance as to whether Charles I should be executed. While the praying went on some functionary proceeded independently with the beheading of the king. The next morning Cromwell said that, since the execution had occurred without its having been ordered, it must have been God's will. This supposes a notion of providence in which God is in total control, either determining all events or selectively determining some events.

The traditionalist says to me, 'You make God limited if he doesn't have that sort of control.' But is God limited if he cannot work any nonsense in the world when he wants to — that is, that he could suddenly create a stone so heavy he could not carry it himself? The imagery leads to absurdity. It is equally absurd to say that we have our own power and freedom (which we all presuppose), but that God can control our action. It is absurd, in other words, to suppose that to do what has to be done, God cannot work within the order of nature, as we have to, but has to destroy his creation to do that. Tillich (1951) says:

> God's directing creativity always creates through the freedom of man and through the spontaneity and structural wholeness of all creatures...Providence is not interference; it is creation... Providence is a *quality* which 'lures' toward fulfilment...The man who believes in providence does not believe that a special divine activity will alter the conditions of finitude and estrangement. He believes, and asserts with the courage of faith, that no situation whatsoever can frustrate the fulfilment of this ultimate destiny, that nothing can separate him from the love of God which is in Christ Jesus (pp. 266-7).

The concept of an all-powerful, almighty, all-controlling God is antithetical to the reality of the world. That concept, despite its widespread acceptance, is an adolescent and immature view of the nature of God's activity. I for one can't believe in a God like that.

On the other hand, the nature of the world is consistent with the concept of God as persuasive love that is never coercive. That in the end is the only sort of power that matters. The form of power that is most admirable is that which empathises with others and empowers them (Cobb 1991b, p. 180).

What then is the promise? It is not that everything will come to a good end. Many things come to a bad end. Faith in divine providence is faith that nothing can prevent us from fulfilling the ultimate meaning of our existence, neither pestilence, nor holocaust, neither persecution nor poverty, neither 'principalities nor powers', dictators nor tyrants. Circumstances need not destroy us. What matters is our attitude to circumstances and that can always be positive, no matter how dire the prospects may seem to be. No person, nor any situation, need ever have an unbreakable grasp upon us. It is the faith that it is possible to act creatively in *any* situation. It is on that level of meaning that the Christian faith makes sense. The lower levels are a threat to both reason and faith.

Every life has two aspects, the objective and the subjective; the impact on us of external circumstance and then our own subjective contribution, our inner dealing with it. It is mainly our inward, subjective contribution that in the end determines what life means to us. 'I have overcome the world', said Jesus. His victory was inward. So it is with us. The founder of Alcoholics Anonymous was a militant agnostic, scornful of religion, he was hopelessly beaten by drink, and then to his amazement, reaching out in his despair for some power to save himself, he found it. He called that resource God. He didn't let the objective facts get him down.

Prayer is not the endeavour to get God to do what we want. It is the endeavour to put ourselves in such a relationship with God that the possibilities of God for our lives become concretely real in our experience. We can believe this can happen yet at the same time we should not minimise the tragedies that beset some lives which seem unredeemable as far as we can tell; the five-year-old bashed to death by his parents, the mentally deficient children abandoned in a bombed-out hospital in Sarajevo. What subjective contribution can redeem their situation unless it be someone coming to the rescue before it is too late? Our task then is to alleviate the situations in which individuals don't have a chance, if we can. But many of our efforts may be frustrated. Socrates pointed out that it is not what others do to us that harms our character. It is what we do to others. And that includes what we do not do to others.

This view of the nature of God's activity is not only a view of the nature of goodness but also of the nature of evil. As Cobb (1969) says:

> If God is understood as that factor in the universe which makes for novelty, life, intensity of feeling, consciousness, freedom, and in man for genuine concern for others, and which provides that measure of order which supports these, we must recognise that he is also responsible in a significant way for the evil of the world. If there were nothing at all or total chaos, or if there were only some very simple structure of order, there would be little evil — there would instead be the absence of both good and evil.

Earthquakes and tornadoes would be neither good nor evil in a world devoid of life. Only where there are significant values does the possibility of their thwarting, their conflict, and their destruction arise. *The possibility of pain is the price paid for consciousness and the capacity for intense feeling* [emphasis added]. Sin exists as the corruption of the capacity for love. Thus God by creating good provides the context within which there is evil (p. 96).

In this view, evil springs not from providence but from freedom and chance. Without these two principles the world is incomprehensible. For God to completely control the world would be to annihilate it.

The world's response to God's feelings for the world

The second proposition about God is: *The only adequate human response to God's persuasive love is infinite passion.*

The previous section was mainly concerned with the divine eros that reaches out to all creatures as an internal relation in their lives. All creatures means not just living organisms such as birds and kangaroos, but all individual entities from protons to people.

Compassion is extended, not only to the lives of our fellow humans but to those species who share the Earth with us that they too may experience a richness in their own lives. Charles Hartshorne (1991) expressed appreciation of E. O. Wilson's book *Biophilia* on the human love of living things but added: 'His mistake is in supposing there is *any* simply non-living and insentient, yet concrete and singular reality' (p. 585). At the age of fifteen, Hartshorne wrote this poem:

> There's a spirit in the mountains,
> In every living thing,
> And it sparkles in the fountains
> That from the hillsides spring...
> It is the spirit of God's love. (1991, p. 692)

Even at that age, he tell us that he was already focusing in this poem on the inner lives of feeling of animals far from the human kind.

In this section we are concerned with the relationship between God and individual entities of the creation as the response of the creature to the divine lure. We best understand the response of the entities of creation to God through the response of the human person. Plato spoke of the only adequate response to the claim of ultimate reality being undimmed and unwearied passion. *Infinite passion* is the phrase Paul Tillich borrowed from Kierkegaard to express the only adequate 'with all' response to God's persuasive love. It is, says Hartshorne (1991), 'to be creative and foster creativity in others' (p. 585).

There is not just one creator but many creators. Indeed the universe is full of creators, yet one is supremely over all, else a multitude of creators would produce chaos. So it is natural that creative human individuals tend to find themselves in the company of those who are similarly creative. This in itself results in coordination. The creative evolution of the cosmos is a consequence of the combined creative activity of the individual entities of the universe.

There are, in the above discussion, two arguments for the existence of God, one from *order*, the other from *novelty*. The new unity in every creative act is no mere rearrangement of things that already existed. The creative person in his or her creativity is becoming a new individual moment by moment, day by day. The idea is applicable to all levels. In Whitehead's phrase, 'the many become one and are increased by one.' This is the nature of the new. In creativity something really novel is added to the universe, though not disjunct from it.

Some kind of tendency to the realisation of further possibilities, some way in which the individual entities of the world lay hold of an order which lies beyond the present, must belong to the individual entities of the world. Otherwise evolution is completely unintelligible.

At the human level this lure is felt as an imperative. The response to the divine lure is passionate. 'I can do no other so help me God', cried Luther when interrogated at the diet of Worms. It was Hume who said that intellect without passion is barren: It is not even a case of choosing this rather than that. It is a case of being grasped by this rather than that. We open our lives to being grasped by something greater than ourselves, which becomes part of ourselves. This is the full meaning of incarnation, literally 'becoming flesh', which is becoming concretely real instead of remaining only a possibility.

Traditional Christianity, since the councils of the third century, has restricted the word incarnation to the presence of God in the life of Jesus. Yet there are numerous examples in the Bible of God as incarnate in all individual entities, such as, for example, the God of 'all things' in Colossians 1:15-20. In these brief five verses the six-times repeated 'all things' affirms that all things subsist in God and through God are subjects of God's persuasive love. God is internally related to all individual entities. This sort of incarnational theology of creation stands in strong contrast to a doctrine of God as the *deus ex machina* who, having made the machinery of the world, left it to look after itself.

The inclusive concept of incarnation has been given strong emphasis in the concept of the world as God's body as developed particularly by Sallie McFague in two books (McFague 1987, 1993). She emphasises the importance of this perspective if Christians today are to really understand what the ecological crisis is all about and how its consequences may be avoided. Sally McFague (1993) speaks of 'radicalising the incarnation', and of God as 'embodied in the world' and adds that it is neither idolatry nor pantheism. The world is not identified or confused with God. Yet it is the place where God is present.

> For our time when we understand human existence in continuity with all other forms of life and hence must think of our relation to God in an ecological context, that mediation is appropriately radicalised and expanded to include the whole cosmos (p. 134).

God's feelings of the world

The third proposition about God is: *God responds to the world with infinite passion.*

It is as true to say the world experiences God as the world is created as to say that God experiences the world as the world is created. God is both cause (in creating the world) and effect (in experiencing the world). God is conceived as process of becoming rather than as static being. By contrast, in the classical view, God is said to be loving, yet without anything like emotion, feeling, or sensitivity to the feelings of others. Aristotle said it first: God is mover of all things, unmoved by any. The God of Aristotle is totally unaffected by what happens in the world. The same is true of the God of Saint Anselm, the God of Saint Thomas Aquinas and the God of the first of the 39 Articles of the Church of England as listed to this day in the back of the Anglican Prayer Book.

At the opposite extreme to Aristotle's God is the polytheistic view in Greek mythology, whose gods are capable of all sorts of emotional feelings; they are jealous, easily offended, desirous sexually and yet immortal.

The mediating view is that God is loving in the sense of feeling, with unique adequacy, the feelings of all others, entirely free from inferior emotions (except as vicariously participated), steadfast in response to the novelties in the creatures with ever-new experiences. God takes into his own life the immediacy of all the currents of feeling, moment by moment. Hartshorne (1948) says:

'He alone not only knows but feels, and finds his own joy in sharing their lives, lived according to their own free decisions, not fully anticipated by any detailed plan of his own' (p. xv). Whatever we do makes a difference to God. The contention is that only such a view can do justice to the biblical message at its best and that, quite apart from the Bible, only such a view is a coherent, intelligible way of conceiving God. A love that leaves the lover unaffected by the joys and sufferings of the one who is loved is not worthy of being called love at all.

It is really quite extraordinary how rarely in traditional Christianity God is conceived to suffer with and rejoice with the creation. God is represented as judging, punishing, sometimes sentencing people to torment. So the inquisitor of today, as of old, would not understand a visitation from the Christ. In his self-righteousness he would say, as Dostoevski had him say to the visiting Christ, 'Why hast thou come now to hinder us?' Real love is neither judgmental nor condemnatory. Instead it comes alongside and experiences the suffering and the joy of the one who is loved. I can believe in a God like that.

The denial of God as one who feels the world's joys and sufferings was largely due to the Greek notion that perfection is immutability: if God is perfect then God cannot be changed in any way by what happens in the world. Such a God is invulnerable to the world's suffering. On the contrary, to be enriched by the enrichment of the world is to be responsive to the world and therefore to be more loving.

Responsiveness is the nature of perfection, not immutability. What, you may ask, is the responsiveness of God to the suffering of 6 million Jews and the ghoulish satisfaction of their executioners? This is not an easy question to deal with and perhaps we would prefer not to ask it. Yet it is a question that we must face if we believe that God feels all the feelings of existence. Could it be that God feels the excruciating suffering of the tormented but he cannot feel satisfaction in the satisfaction of their tormentors? God feels their satisfactions and is tormented by them.

God's creative activity inspires the individual entities of creation to themselves be creative. Their experiences are saved in the experience of God. In Whitehead's (1978) language: 'What is done in the world is transformed into a reality in heaven' (p. 351). In the sentence that follows he says 'and the reality in heaven passes back into the world'. This is an interesting speculation that the world not only makes a difference to God but that the difference to God floods back into the world as new possibilities for the world. 'In this way', says John Buchanan (1994), 'a flow of feeling is established between God and the creatures, a flow which enriches both' (p. 594). Buchanan refers to this as the *cosmic dance* of the Whiteheadian cosmos that holds within itself zest, novelty, adventure and peace.

In this vision of a deity who is not a supreme autocrat, but a universal agent of persuasion and responsiveness, whose 'power is the worship he inspires' (Whitehead), who feels all the feelings of the world, some of us find not only a new way of understanding the world but a new way of facing the tasks of today.

Conclusion

The proposition of this chapter is that the universal existence of subjectivity in the individual entities of creation requires the existence of cosmic mind at the heart of the universe.

Cosmic mind or God is not conceived as an omnipotent, supernatural, legalistic ruler of the universe. Cosmic mind is not supernatural but natural.

God acts in the world by compassionate persuasive love, never by coercion. Individual entities from protons to people experience God through their internal relations. This is the nature of the 'within of things'. God acts by being 'felt' by the individual entities of the creation as they take account of their environment internally. For us humans this is experienced as values and purposes. God is not the sole cause of all happenings. God's causality is always exercised in relation to individual entities that have their own measure of self-determination. So divine purpose is a preferable description, not divine design. The latter gives the impression of a preordained blueprint, whereas the future is open-ended. Likewise, the word providence is misleading if it suggests a divine planning in which everything is predetermined. However, it is appropriate in the meaning that there is a creative and saving possibility in every situation which cannot be destroyed by any event. Created goods are destroyed but not creative good.

The only adequate human response to God's persuasive love is infinite passion. The proposition is that all actual entities experience the divine persuasion and that the only appropriate response on the part of humans is with infinite passion. It is the response to divine persuasion that gives order to the societies of individual entities from protons to people. And this ordering leads to novelty in the creative process.

God responds to the world with infinite passion. It is as true to say that the world experiences God as the world is created as to say that God experiences the world as it is created. God is both cause (in creating the world) and effect (in experiencing the world). The God of Aristotle and of classical theism is totally unaffected by what happens in the world. The God of process thought feels with unique adequacy the feelings of all others. A love that gives but does not respond to the joys and sufferings of the world is not worthy of being called love at all. Responsiveness, not immutability, is the nature of perfection.

REFERENCES

Agar, W. E. (1943; 1951 rev. ed) *A Contribution to the Theory of the Living Organism* Melbourne: Melbourne University Press.

Armstrong, David (1979) 'The nature of mind' in *The Mind-Brain Identity Theory* (ed. C. V. Borst) London: Macmillan.

Barbour, Ian G. (1990) *Religion in an Age of Science: The Gifford Lectures 1989-91*, Vol. 1, London: SCM.

Beecher, H. K. (1956) 'Relation of significance of wound to pain experienced' *J. Amer. Med. Assn.* 161, pp. 1609-13.

Berman, M. (1981) *The Reenchantment of the World* Ithaca, NY: Cornell University Press.

Birch, Charles (1990) *On Purpose* Kensington: New South Wales University Press.

Birch, Charles (1993) *Regaining Compassion: For humanity and nature* Kensington: New South Wales University Press.

Birch, Charles & Cobb, John B. Jr (1981) *The Liberation of Life: From the cell to the commmunity* Cambridge University Press. Reprinted 1990 Denton, TX: Environmental Ethics Books.

Birch, Charles, Eakin, William & McDaniel, Jay B. (eds) (1990) *Liberating Life: Contemporary approaches to ecological theology* Maryknoll, NY: Orbis.

Boden, Margaret (1990) *The Creative Mind: Myth and mechanisms* London: Weidenfeld & Nicholson.

Bohm, David (1982) 'David Bohm: An interview by Robert Temple' *New Scientist* 96 pp. 361-5.

Braude, Stephen (1991) *First Person Plural: Multiple personality and the philosophy of mind* New York: Routledge.

Brock, Rita Nakashima (1988) *Journeys of the Heart: A christology of erotic power* New York: Crossroad.

Buchanan, John (1944) *Universal Feeling: Whitehead and psychology* PhD thesis, Atlanta: Emory University.

Bullock, Alan (1993) *Hitler and Stalin: Parallel lives* London: Fontana.

Burton, Maurice (1978) *Just Like an Animal* London: J. M. Dent.

Cavalieri, Paola & Singer, Peter (eds) (1993) *The Great Ape Project: Equality beyond humanity*. London: Fourth Estate.

Chalmers, D. J. (1995) *Toward a Theory of Consciousness* Cambridge MA: MIT Press.

Cheney, Dorothy L. & Seyfarth, Robert M. (1990) *How Monkeys See the World: Inside the mind of another species* Chicago: University of Chicago Press.

Clark, Kenneth (1969) *Civilization: A personal view* London: BBC and John Murray.

Cobb, John B. Jr (1969) *God and the World* Philadelphia: Westminster.

Cobb, John B. Jr (1984) 'Overcoming reductionism' in *Existence and Actuality: Conversations with Charles Hartshorne* (eds John B. Cobb Jr & F. I. Gamwell) Chicago: University of Chicago Press.

Cobb, John B. Jr (1991a) *Matters of Life and Death* Louisville, KY: Westminster/ John Knox.

Cobb, John B. Jr (1991b) 'Hartshorne's Importance for theology' in *The Philosophy of Charles Hartshorne* (ed. Lewis Edwin Hahn) pp. 169-83 La Salle, IL: Open Court.

Cobb, John B. Jr (1992) 'The Cosmos and God: The dependence of science on faith' The Templeton Lecture, University of Sydney, University of Edinburgh Press.

Cobb, John B. Jr (1995) *Is it too late?: A theology of ecology* Denton TX: Environmental Ethics Books.

Cobb, John B. and Griffin, David Ray (1976) *Process Theology: An introductory exposition* Philadelphia: Westminster.

Cookson, Clive (1993, September 11) 'Calling Dr Dalek — your patient is waiting' London, *Financial Times* p. 4.

Cornwell, John (1994, July 2) 'Behind the Mind' *The Tablet* pp. 829-30.

Crick, Francis (1994) *The Astonishing Hypothesis: The scientific search for the soul* New York: Scribner's.

Cronin, Helena (1992, November 1) 'What do animals want?' *New York Times Book Review* p. 14.

Damasio, Antonio R. (1994) *Descartes' Error: Emotion, reason and the human brain* New York: Grosset/Putnam.

Davidson, Clive (1993, March 27) 'I process therefore I am' *New Scientist* 137 pp. 22-7.

Davies, Paul (1992) *The Mind of God: Science and the search for ultimate meaning* New York: Simon & Schuster.

Davies, Paul & Gribbin, John (1991) *The Matter Myth: Towards 21st-century science* London: Viking.

Dawkins, Marian Stamp (1980) *Animal Suffering* London: Chapman & Hall.

Dawkins, Marian Stamp (1993) *Through our Eyes Only?: The search for animal consciousness* New York: W. H. Freeman/Spektrum.

Delbruck, Max (1986) *Mind from Matter: An essay in evolutionary epistemology* Oxford: Blackwell Scientific Publications.

Dennett, Daniel C. (1991) *Consciousness Explained* Boston: Little Brown.

Denton, Derek (1993) *The Pinnacle of Life: Consciousness and self-awareness in humans and animals* St Leonards, NSW: Allen & Unwin.

Dobzhansky, Th (1967) *The Biology of Ultimate Concern* New York: New American Library.

Donnelly, Strachan & Nolan, Kathleen (eds) (1990, May/June) 'Animal science and ethics' *The Hastings Report Special Supplement.*

Dyson, Freeman (1988) *Infinite in all Directions* New York: Harper & Row.

Easlea, Brian (1973) *Liberation and the Aims of Science: An essay on the obstacles to the building of a beautiful world* London: Chatto & Windus.

Edelman, Gerald M. (1992) *Bright Air, Brilliant Fire: On the matter of mind* New York: Basic Books.

Gazzaniga, Michael S. (1988) *Mind and Matter: How mind and brain interact to create our conscious lives* Boston: Houghton Mifflin.

Gelernter, David (1994) *The Muse in the Machine: Computers and creative thought* London: Fourth Estate/Free Press.

Gingerich, Owen (1994) 'A Mind in Motion' *Nature* 369 p. 195.

Goodall, Jan van Lawick (1971) *In the Shadow of Man* Boston: Houghton Mifflin.

Goodall, Jan van Lawick (1986) *The Chimpanzees of Gombe: Patterns of behavior* Cambridge, MA: Harvard University Press.

Griffin, David Ray (ed.) (1988) *The Reenchantment of Science: Postmodern proposals* Albany, NY: State University of New York Press.

Griffin, David Ray (1990) 'The restless universe: A postmodern vision' in *The Restless Earth*, Nobel Conference xxiv (ed. K. J. Carlson) pp. 59-111 San Francisco: Harper & Row.

Griffin, David Ray (ed.) (1993) *Founders of Constructive Postmodern Philosophy: Peirce, James, Bergson, Whitehead and Hartshorne* Albany, NY: State University of New York Press.

Griffin, David Ray (1995) *Unsnarling the World-Knot: Consciousness, freedom and the mind-body problem* (in press).

Griffin, Donald R. (1981) *The Question of Animal Awareness* New York: Rockefeller University Press.

Griffin, Donald R. (1984) *Animal Thinking* Cambridge, MA: Harvard University Press.

Griffin, Donald R. (1992) *Animal Minds* Chicago: University of Chicago Press.

Haldane, J. S. (1935) *The Philosophy of a Biologist* Oxford: Oxford University Press.

Hampson, Norman (1990) *The Enlightenment: An evaluation of its assumptions, attitudes and values* Harmondsworth: Penguin Books.

Hardy, Alister (1965) *The Living Stream* London: Collins.

Harrison, Harry & Minsky, Marvin (1992) *The Turing Option* New York: Warner.

Hartshorne, Charles (1934) *The Philosophy and Psychology of Sensation* Chicago: University of Chicago Press.

Hartshorne, Charles (1948) *The Divine Relativity: A social conception of God* New Haven, CT: Yale University Press.

Hartshorne, Charles (1973) *Born to Sing: An interpretation and world survey of bird song* Bloomington, IN: Indiana University Press.

Hartshorne, Charles (1987) *Wisdom as Moderation: A philosophy of the middle way* Albany, NY: State University of New York Press.

Hartshorne, Charles (1991) 'A Reply to my critics' in *The Philosophy of Charles Hartshorne* (ed. Lewis Edwin Hahn) pp. 569-731, The Library of Living Philosophers xx, La Salle, IL: Open Court.

Himmelfarb, Gertrude (1994) *On Looking into the Abyss: Untimely thoughts on culture and society* New York: Alfred A. Knopf.

Hinde, R.A. (1969) *Bird Vocalizations: Their relation to current problems in biology and psychology* Cambridge: Cambridge University Press.

Hodgson, David (1991) *The Mind Matters: Consciousness and choice in a quantum world* Oxford: Clarendon Press.

Holroyd, Stuart (1989). *The Arkana Dictionary of New Perspectives* New York: Arkana.

Kauffman, Stuart A. (1993) *The Origins of Order: Self-organisation and selection in evolution* Oxford: Oxford University Press.

Kearney, Hugh (1971) *Science and Change 1500–1700* New York: McGraw Hill.

Kihlstrom, J. F. (1993) 'The psychological unconscious and the self' in *Experimental Studies and Theoretical Studies of Consciousness* (eds Gregory R. Bock & Joan Marsh) pp. 147-56 New York: Wiley-Interscience.

Klaaren, Eugene (1977) *Religious Origins of Modern Science* Washington, DC: University Press of America.

Lepore, Ernst & van Gulick, Robert (eds) (1991) *John Searle and his critics* Oxford: Basil Blackwell.

Lewin, Roger (1994) 'Birth of a human robot' *New Scientist* 1925, 14 May pp. 26-30.

Lewontin, R. C. (1991) *Biology as Ideology: The doctrine of DNA* New York: Harper Perennial.

Madell, Geoffrey (1988) *Mind and Materialism* Edinburgh: The University Press.

McDaniel, Jay B. (1989) *Of God and Pelicans: A theology of reverence for life* Louisville, KY: Westminster/John Knox.

McFague, Sally (1987) *Models of God: Theology for an ecological, nuclear age* Philadelphia: Fortress.

McFague, Sally (1993) *The Body of God: An ecological theology* Philadelphia: Fortress.

McGinn, Colin (1991) *The Problem of Consciousness: Essays towards a resolution* Oxford: Basil Blackwell.

McGinn, Colin (1993) 'Consciousness and cosmology: hyperdualism ventilated' in *Consciousness: Psychological and philosophical essays* (eds Martin Davies & Glyn W. Humphreys) pp. 155-77 Oxford: Basil Blackwell.

Merchant, Caroline (1980) *The Death of Nature: Women, ecology and the scientific revolution* San Francisco: Harper & Row.

Mestel, Rosie (1994) 'Let mind talk' *New Scientist* 1935, 23 July pp. 26-31.

Midgley, Mary (1983) *Animals and Why they Matter: A journey around the species barrier* Harmondsworth: Penguin.

Morgan, C. L. (1923) *Emergent Evolution* London: Willis & Norgate.

Nagel, Thomas (1974) 'What is it like to be a bat?' *Philosophical Review* 83: pp. 435-50. Reprinted in *Mortal Questions* 1979 (Thomas Nagel) Cambridge University Press.

Nash, Roderick (1990) *The Rights of Nature: A history of environmental ethics* Leichhardt, NSW: Primavera Press.

Nuland, Sherwin B. (1994) 'The pill of pills' *New York Review of Books* 41 (11), pp. 4-8.

Ogden, Schubert M. (1967) *The Reality of God* London: SCM.

Pagels, Heinz (1988) *The Dreams of Reason* New York: Simon & Schuster.

Passmore, John (1975) 'The treatment of animals' *Journal of the History of Ideas* 36 pp. 195-218.

Pinches, Charles & McDaniel, Jay B. (eds) (1993) *Good News for Animals: Christian approaches to animal well-being* Maryknoll, NY: Orbis.

Popper, K. R. & Eccles, J. C. (1977) *The Self and its Brain* Berlin: Springer-Verlag.

Prigogine, Ilya & Stengers, Isabelle (1984) *Order and Chaos: Man's new dialogue with nature* New York: Bantam Books.

Rachels, James (1990) *Created from Animals: The moral implications of Darwinism* Oxford: Oxford University Press.

Regan, Tom (1983) *The Case for Animal Rights* Berkeley: University of California Press.

Rey, Georges (1993) 'Sensational Sentences' in *Consciousness: Psychological and philosophical essays* (eds Martin Davies & G. W. Humphreys) pp. 240-57 Oxford: Basil Blackwell

Rollin, Bernard E. (1989) *The Unheeded Cry: Animal consciousness, animal pain and science* Oxford: Oxford University Press.

Rose, Steven (1995) 'The rise of neurogenetic determinism' *Nature* 373 pp. 380-2.

Sackville-West (1992, July 12) 'Love's Faded Tokens' *New York Times Book Review* p. 35.

Sapolsky, Robert M. (1994) *Why Zebras don't get Ulcers: A guide to stress, stress-related diseases, and coping* New York: W. H. Freeman.

Seager, William (1991) *Metaphysics of Consciousness* New York: Routledge.

Searle, John R. (1980) 'Minds, brains and programs' *Behavioural and Brain Sciences* 3 pp. 417-24.

Searle, John R. (1992) *The Rediscovery of Mind* Cambridge, MA: MIT Press.

Seyfarth, Robert M. & Cheney, Dorothy L. (1992) 'Meaning and mind in monkeys' *Scientific American* 257 (6) pp. 78-84.

Sheldrake, Rupert (1990) *The Rebirth of Nature: The greening of science and God* London: Century.

Singer, Peter (1976) *Animal Liberation: A new ethics for our treatment of animals* London: Jonathan Cape. Revised edition 1991 London: Avon.

Smart, J. J. C. (1979) 'Sensations and brain processes' in *The Mind-Brain Identity Theory* (ed. C. V. Borst) London: Macmillan.

Sorabji, Richard (1993) *Animal Minds and Human Morals: The origins of the Western debate* London: Duckworth.

Sperry, Roger W. (1992a) 'Paradigms of belief, theory and metatheory' *Zygon* 27 pp. 245-59.

Sperry, Roger W. (1992b) 'Turnabout on consciousness: A mentalist view' *The Science of Mind and Behavior* 13 pp. 259-80.

Strawson, Galen (1994) *Mental Reality* Cambridge MA: MIT Press.

Sutherland, Stuart (1985) 'Consciousness beyond ourselves' *Nature* 313 p. 410.

Tennov, Dorothy (1979) *Love and Limerance: The experience of being in love* New York: Stein and Day.

Thomas, Elizabeth (1994) 'Of ivory and the survival of elephants' *The New York Review of Books* 41(6) pp. 3-6.

Tillich, Paul (1951) *Systematic Theology* Volume 1, Chicago: University of Chicago Press.

Tillich, Paul (1953) *The Shaking of the Foundations* New York: Charles Scribner's Sons.

Torrey, E., Taylor, E., Bowler, A. & Gottesman, I. (1993) *Schizophrenia and Manic-depressive Disorder* New York: Basic Books.

Vines, Gail (1993) 'Planet of the free apes?' *New Scientist* 138 pp. 39-42.

Walsh, Anthony (1991) *The Science of Love: Understanding love and its effects on mind and body* New York: Prometheus Books.

Weizenbaum, J. (1976) *Computer Power and Human Reason: From judgment to calculation* San Francisco: Freeman.

Whitehead, A. N. (1929) *The Function of Reason* Boston: Beacon.

Whitehead, A. N. (1930) *Religion in the Making* Cambridge: Cambridge University Press.

Whitehead, A. N. (1933) *Science and the Modern World* Cambridge: Cambridge University Press.

Whitehead, A. N. (1942) *Adventure of Ideas* Harmondsworth: Penguin.

Whitehead, A. N. (1966) *Modes of Thought* New York: Free Press.

Whitehead, A. N. (1978) *Process and Reality* (corrected edition, eds D. R. Griffin & D. W. Sherbourne) New York: Free Press (original edition 1929).

Wieman, Henry N. (1947) *The Source of Human Good* Chicago: University of Chicago Press.

Wilber, Ken (1984) *Quantum Questions,* New Science Library, Boulder: Shambhala.

Willey, Basil (1953) *The Seventeenth Century Background* New York: Doubleday Anchor Books.

Witham, Larry (1995, 23 April) 'Physicians research ecstasy as cure for addicts' *The Washington Times* p. A3.

Wright, Sewall (1964) 'Biology and the philosophy of science' in *Process and Divinity* (eds W. L. Reese & E. Freeman) pp. 102-25, La Salle, IL: Open Court.

Yates, Frances A. (1972) *The Rosicrucian Enlightenment* London: Routledge & Kegan Paul.

INDEX